CHAMPIONSHIP
BASKETBALL

TOP COLLEGE COACHES PRESENT THEIR WINNING STRATEGIES, TIPS, AND TECHNIQUES FOR PLAYERS AND COACHES

CHAMPIONSHIP BASKETBALL

TOP COLLEGE COACHES PRESENT THEIR WINNING STRATEGIES, TIPS, AND TECHNIQUES FOR PLAYERS AND COACHES

By Roland Lazenby with David Meador and Ed Green

CONTEMPORARY
BOOKS, INC.
CHICAGO ▪ NEW YORK

Library of Congress Cataloging-in-Publication Data

Lazenby, Roland.
    Championship basketball.

    1. Basketball.   I. Meador, David.   II. Green, Ed.
III. Title.
GV885.L38   1987   796.32'363   86-29375
ISBN 0-8092-4874-3

Published by Contemporary Books, Inc.
180 North Michigan Avenue, Chicago, Illinois 60601
Manufactured in the United States of America
Library of Congress Catalog Card Number: 86-29375
International Standard Book Number: 0-8092-4874-3

Published simultaneously in Canada by Beaverbooks, Ltd.
195 Allstate Parkway, Valleywood Business Park
Markham, Ontario L3R 4T8 Canada

This book is dedicated to John Wooden, the ultimate champion.

CONTENTS

ACKNOWLEDGMENTS

Karen Lazenby spent many hours typing and editing this manuscript. The Patrick Henry High School (Roanoke, Va.) varsity players—Ronnie Pendleton, Curtis Blair, Melvin Davis, Brian Combs, Tony Dudley, George Lynd, Bernard Basham, and Todd Evans—gave freely of their time to serve as models for instructional photography.

Special thanks to Patrick Henry Coach Woody Deans. Also serving as models were Andy Gray of Hampden-Sydney College and Gerald Holmes, a professional playing overseas. Howard Garfinkel of Five Star Camps graciously allowed us to observe his camp at Radford University.

Chuck Person, Auburn University.

INTRODUCTION

Basketball is an exceptional game. Perhaps more than any other sport, it demands physical and mental completeness.

The requirements for success are very clear. First, a player must understand his skills, abilities, and limitations. Then he and his coach must work at weaving his talent with that of four other players into a team. Few other sports require such a high level of integration of the individual player with the team.

In basketball, that melding of player and team is the ultimate goal. Likewise, it is an ultimate challenge, a continual, elusive riddle. The search for team chemistry is a constant one for all coaches and players. It is conducted in the midst of a fast-paced game in the midst of a fast-paced season.

Whether the game is a pick-up shoot-out or the NCAA Finals, that challenge remains the same. A group of five players must establish order amidst chaos. Their success depends on the economy and efficiency of the order they establish.

Perhaps the basic elements of basket-ball can best be illustrated in a pick-up game. Five strangers sign up to take on the winners in a YMCA Saturday afternoon game. Five who have never played together must quickly become a team. They do so silently for the most part, relying on signals and quick decisions. The forwards naturally go to the front court, the guards to the perimeter. The oncoming players size up their opponents and select their defensive assignments. Once into the game, they must determine who has the hot hand, who will take the task of rebounding, who will hang back and guard the fast break.

Playground basketball becomes the art of quick assembly, a beautiful system of natural selection. Those who put together a team rapidly will usually win and keep playing. The five players who combine talent and team survive. Those who fail to do so must sit on the sidelines, wait their next turn, and think about where they failed.

Sometimes the pure talent of a single

player can overpower anything a team might accomplish. But the odds always favor the group. Five men can beat one just about any day of the week.

In structured basketball, there is a strong element of the playground's art of quick assembly. But at each level of amateur competition, the game becomes more complex, more reliant on the individual's understanding of himself and his team.

That relationship between the team and the individual player is the intriguing essence of basketball. It also is the focus of this book, *Championship Basketball.*

We asked several major-college coaches to define a complete player and a complete team. Many were generous enough to share their basketball wisdom with us. In addition, we have added a selection of basic tips, drills, and plays to help teams and individuals develop and grow.

John Wooden once said, "There is a very fine line between the champion and the runner-up." We hope this book helps you find that line and cross it, whether you're a player or a coach, whether you're fighting for a championship or just struggling to survive to the next game at the YMCA.

NCAA championship game, 1986.

Johnny Dawkins (right), Duke University.

1
THE COMPLETE PLAYER

John Wooden, the master of championships, says three things are vital to success in basketball—fundamentals, conditioning, and teamwork.

That logic applies to most sports, but even more so to basketball. Great teams are built with fundamentally sound, complete players. Thus, the first step for a would-be champion is making a sincere commitment to becoming a complete player.

With that in mind, we asked some of the best college coaches in the country to give us their definitions of a complete player. Many of them responded with spare, concise definitions.

For example, Gene Bartow, of the University of Alabama–Birmingham, said, "A complete player is sound fundamentally, has a great feel for winning games, and provides leadership on and off the court."

Charlie Moir, of Viginia Tech, was even more terse: "Larry Bird" was his answer.

Gene Bartow, University of Alabama-Birmingham.

But Duke's Mike Krzyzewski said young players shouldn't think that being a complete player means simply being the team's star and big scorer. "A complete player doesn't have to be a starter. He can be a seventh or eighth man. In fact, he may not have the skill level to be a star. Some people use the term 'complete player' as a synonym for a star. But I look at it as a kid who is maximizing his potential.

"Players such as a Larry Bird or a Johnny Dawkins have such a level of talent that they don't have to be complete players to be stars. The fact that they are complete players says quite a bit about their characters. Players like Bird or Dawkins are complete because they will use whatever phase of the game it takes to win—rebounding, shooting, passing.

Johnny Dawkins, Duke University.

"The complete player should have the ability to pass, play defense, shoot, and play within the team concept, maximizing his individual skills to where he doesn't take away from the team concept. The mental aspect of that is paramount as far as his importance to the overall team concept. The team concept can't be disrupted."

Krzyzewski said that at the core of the complete player is "a determination to win. He is able to test his abilities on the line every night without being afraid of failure.

"The complete player has an effect on the game in so many areas. He may not necessarily score. He may be a passer or a screener. He doesn't care about stats. He understands the whole game. That's why I think the mental part of the game, the intelligence, is so important."

Becoming a complete player begins with self-understanding: knowing how you fit into the team picture, and then determining how to broaden your game for the benefit of the team.

Self-understanding begins with setting your own goals for improvement or, better yet, preparing your own definition of a complete player. In so doing, you might want to hear some other coaches' definitions:

Jerry Pimm, of the University of California–Santa Barbara: "A complete player is one who has control of his mental capacities, is quick of foot, can read defenses, and is obviously under control at all times."

Jim Harrick, of Pepperdine: "Complete, to me, means fundamental—down in a stance offensively and defensively, the ability to jump-stop on balance and under control. A complete player uses his hands and arms. He denies on defense. He can shoot, rebound, defend, and run the floor."

Sonny Smith, of Auburn: "A player will-

Sonny Smith (left), Auburn University.

ing to lose himself in the group for the good of the group. A player fundamentally sound with physical and mental capabilities that drive him to be better than he is."

Johnny Orr, of Iowa State: "One that performs all the skills—dribbling, passing, shooting, rebounding, and playing defense—the complete fundamental player."

Glen Wilkes, of Stetson University: "A complete player is one who possesses well-rounded fundamental skills and combines them with the proper attitude and a thorough knowledge of the game.

"A complete player is strong both offensively and defensively. He can shoot, pass, drive, rebound, and can play defense both as an individual and in the team concept.

"A complete player possesses an attitude that will generate team play among his teammates. He is unselfish, enthusiastic, and positive.

"A complete player takes years to develop. A coach makes a contribution to his development by teaching basic fundamental skills in practice, stressing the importance of attitude and team play."

Bobby Cremins, of Georgia Tech: "A complete player has good skills, a knowledge of the game, and an attitude for hard work. He must accept his role. Also, he must maintain academic requirements and deal with setbacks in a positive manner."

Developing into a complete player involves a great deal of hard work. The difficult task for most young players is discovering their strengths and learning how to use them in competition. Just as important is confronting their weaknesses and dedicating themselves to eliminating them.

That's easy enough to say but very difficult to do. For many players, finding a basketball niche can be a lifelong process. The Houston Rockets' Ralph Sampson, for example, is 7'4" and is tremendously

The Complete Player

strong and agile, but no player has had a more complicated search for a playing identity.

Sampson was incredibly thin as a fast-growing adolescent in Harrisonburg, Virginia. Fortunately, his high school coach, Roger Bergey, recognized Sampson's potential long before he ever reached varsity level.

The coaches worked intensely with Sampson, encouraging him not to be just another awkward big man. There were agility drills, foot drills, pivoting work, even full-court one-on-one drills to make young Ralph a better ball handler.

Only a tall person can relate to the pain and embarrassment of being a tall, skinny, and awkward teenager. Sampson's coaches at Harrisonburg High and the University of Virginia helped him through that experience. As a result, Sampson developed into a marvelously gifted athlete—lean, strong, agile, able to dribble and take jump shots as well as play inside with most other big men.

The problem was that many fans and basketball analysts thought Sampson should spend more time being a center and less time dribbling the ball and attempting jump shots from the top of the key. The criticism was loud during Sampson's years at Virginia. During one semester he took a seminar called "The Psychology of the Gifted Athlete" with Dr. Bob Rotella, the university's acclaimed sports psychologist. Sampson and Dr. Rotella discussed fans' high expectations of their sports heroes. Rotella emphasized that sports figures must not get caught up in those expectations but must establish their own values.

The course helped Sampson realize that he had to pursue his own standards of how the position of center should be played. He knew he had to rebound, play defense, block shots, and do the things

Johnny Dawkins, Duke University.

that all centers did. But he also wanted to incorporate the flexibility of the other positions into his play at center. He wanted to be an adroit ball handler, a sure perimeter shooter, an excellent passer.

Sampson is still determined to bring all those qualities to his game, despite the criticism from fans and coaches that he is trying to do too much. Only time will tell if he has found his true playing identity.

For guards and forwards, the game is less structured, but the path to becoming a complete player is still complicated and difficult. Success awaits only those athletes who aren't lulled into false security by their egos.

Johnny Dawkins is a prime example. He arrived at Duke University in 1982 as a hot-shooting high school blue chipper. As with most high schoolers, he had few defensive skills. But unlike many big-name players, Dawkins had a genuine desire to improve every phase of his game. He practiced incredibly hard to learn defense from Coach Krzyzewski. Normally a shooting guard, Dawkins was forced to play the point his first year at Duke. Ball handling wasn't his strongest suit, but Dawkins rose to the challenge.

By his senior year, he was a legitimate All-American, a player with the savvy to drive, rebound, play defense, do whatever necessary to help his team win. Yet he knew his long-range jump shot was the weak part of his game. He spent the summer before his senior year lifting weights and shooting hundreds of shots each day. That effort paid off as Dawkins led his team to the NCAA Championship Finals.

Johnny Dawkins set his own standards as a complete player. For him, for all the truly great players, improvement and perfection of the game is a lifelong process, a commitment to excellence.

Learn to be your own judge. Listen to others but develop your own strong beliefs about how you should play the game.

Above all, don't forget that your team must come first.

John Wooden (left) with Walt Hazzard, University of California-Los Angeles.

2
THE COMPLETE TEAM

What is the special formula, the special chemistry, that makes a team realize its potential? What is that something special that melds a dozen players into a championship unit?

Should every championship team have a seven-footer at the post? A prototype bruiser at power forward to do the rebounding? A wheeler and dealer at the point? A defensive specialist? A silky smooth shooting guard?

Again, we asked the nation's top coaches for their opinion. Walt Hazzard of UCLA offered us an intriguing answer, recalling his days with the 1964 Bruins, the first of John Wooden's national championship teams.

"I think of chemistry, I think of people accepting their roles," Hazzard said when asked about a complete team. "I think of the 1964 Bruins who went 30-0 with no starter larger than 6′5″.

"The chemistry of that ball club was incredible. First, the architect was John Wooden, the philosopher of basketball. He found five players who liked his style, who were extremely competitive and were winners, and accepted their roles with pride.

"My role was the leader, the spirit of the team. I had come from a great basketball tradition in high school in Philadelphia, where I had been a scorer. At UCLA, I became the playmaker and offensive quarterback. I accepted that role. I knew I could have been the leading scorer, but Gail Goodrich was a great scorer. If he missed five in a row, that was no big deal to him. He would just hit the next five. He was a hungry guy who liked to score points. The other players on the team realized that in the fast-break situations, if he was the guy in the middle, he was gonna take the shot.

"Jack Hirsch, a 6′3″ forward, was our top defender, always assigned to the other team's top scorer. He had the instincts,

John Wooden, University of California-Los Angeles (retired).

the tenacity. He knew how to shut a guy down. In junior college he had averaged 38 points a game, but at UCLA he was the defender.

"Fred Slaughter, our 6'5" center, weighed about 250 pounds. He was ideal for the high-post offense John Wooden ran. Even with that size, he was the high school 100-yard dash champion in Kansas. He played up front on our press, but when the ball crossed half court, he'd still beat everybody back.

"That's what was so brilliant about Coach Wooden. He took the strengths of his individual players and adjusted his system to maximize those abilities.

"Keith Erickson, at 6'5", was our fifth man on the 2–2–1 press. He was a great player, an athlete with great reactions, a great rebounder with excellent timing. Above all, he was a fierce competitor.

"To that, Wooden added his two players off the bench, Kenny Washington and Doug McIntosh. Coach Wooden just fit all these pieces together to make a great team."

Of course there have been many other great championship teams in NCAA history, including several others coached by Wooden. The main point is that each team found its unique combination, its championship chemistry. Seldom has it been by a formula, but rather a mixture of talent, character, role play, and sacrifice.

Occasionally, championship chemistry has been an almost magical, momentary thing. For a few weeks, an unspectacular team will come together and play with confident abandon. Such teams seem to be chosen, predetermined champions. The media call them Cinderellas. North Carolina State's remarkable championship drive in 1983 and Villanova's surprise win in 1985 are the perfect examples.

The lesson seems to be that championship chemistry is a fragile, elusive thing.

The recipe requires plenty of hard work with a healthy supply of luck. The other ingredients vary from situation to situation.

Here's what some of the nation's better coaches look for in building a complete team:

Jerry Pimm: "A team that knows its limitations, knows its strengths and weaknesses, and can play to those limitations."

For the complete player, the adage is "know thyself." For the player on the complete team, the adage becomes "know thy teammates."

Gene Bartow has more specific requirements: "A complete team must have very sound guard play with a good inside game. I think you need a true power forward; a center who can block shots and can intimidate on defense; a good outside-shooting forward; and guards who have great feel for taking care of the basketball and being winners."

Duke's Mike Krzyzewski wonders if there is such a thing as a complete team. Perhaps, he says, it's the NBA All-Star team. Reconsidering, he defines it as "a team that comes closest to maximizing its potential."

With that, Krzyzewski adds that he's opposed to categorizing players as guards, forwards, or centers. "I hope we can have a system where players can develop their total potential, not just fill in positions. I've never figured out why we call our players guards, forwards, or centers. In football or baseball, it's easier to see the positions players occupy. In basketball, where the action is continuous, people aren't just filling a position on the court, they're playing a role."

And for the Duke coach, the broader that role, the better. For that reason, his teams play a lot of man defense and a free-moving offense. "We have a positionless

Jerry Pimm (right) with Conner Henry, University of California-Santa Barbara.

The Complete Team   14

offense," he says. "Our people have the flexibility of playing a number of areas on the court. We have continuous movement, continuous setting of screens. We can have set plays, but not often. We seek a flexibility, based on our players being free to read the opponent's defense and take what advantage that defense gives us."

Glen Wilkes wants everything for his complete team, "one that plays at both ends of the floor. It combines the ability to run, shoot, pass, and defend, with an attitude that fosters team play. This requires players to place the good of the team above their individual goals. Players do not criticize each other, are unselfish, enthusiastic, and positive in their relationships and in their play on the court."

Jim Harrick says a "complete team is a balanced team, all five players scoring in double figures: a fine guard defender, a front line defender, a good ballhandler, a good rebounder, all of them running the floor, being unselfish, sharing the ball. None of them should care who gets the credit."

Sonny Smith adds that he wanted "unrelenting, driven" players "with killer instincts" on his team.

The journey to becoming a complete team, a great team, is the most frustrating, yet also the most fulfilling facet of the game. The search for the complete team is uncharted. Finding what works is up to you, your teammates, and your coach. Good luck.

Bobby Clark, Loyola University of Chicago.

3
FUNDAMENTALS

Birds are born to fly and fish gotta swim, but basketball players are not born; they are made. Even superlative players have had to work on the fundamental skills of the game.

Before you can even dream of scoring 30 points a game or making an eye-popping behind-the-back pass, you've got to feel comfortable and confident on the basketball court. A first step is to get your body accustomed to moving like a basketball player.

Stance. To move quickly and fluidly on the basketball court, you need to assume a basketball stance. A proper basketball stance keeps your body in balance and lets you react to the play on the court. Distribute your weight equally on both feet, but don't stand flat-footed. By keeping your weight forward on the balls of your feet, you will be ready to front your man on defense or move for a pass on offense. It is very important to keep your

Stance.

knees bent; standing with your knees locked will inhibit agility. Keep your head up and be alert.

A balanced stance is particularly important when you play defense. You don't know what the offensive player will do, so you must be ready to react to his movement or your man will blow by you. When you are playing man-to-man defense, assume a boxer's stance: feet wide apart and one foot slightly in front of the other. When you are guarding a man closely, it may be helpful to shift your weight toward your forward foot, so that you will be ready to push off it and move back to prevent your man from driving the baseline. The classic defensive stance resembles the position of a person lowering himself into a chair: knees bent, back straight, feet slightly staggered, head up, and arms held close to the body.

Jump-Stop. Keeping your body under control at all times is basic to good basketball. Beginning players often have a hard time maintaining control when they try to stop running. Their momentum prevents them from coming to a sudden stop, and they shuffle and slide their feet to maintain their balance. A good exercise to help you stop under control is the jump-stop.

As you come down court, stop by planting both your feet firmly on the floor parallel to each other. This way you will be able to stop quickly without sliding and your weight will be distributed evenly on both feet. You will have good balance and be ready to make your next move.

Pivot. Another basic basketball skill is the pivot. When you pivot, think of your pivot foot as being nailed to the floor as you swing your body around it. On offense, moving your pivot foot once it is planted is a traveling violation and will result in a turnover. Move your free foot in the direction away from the defender, keeping your body between him and the ball. You will

Pivot 1.

Pivot 2.

find that pivoting is also a vital defensive skill, when you attempt to block out your opponent on a rebound.

Because pivoting requires shifting your weight almost entirely to your pivot foot, it is easy to lose your balance. Practice by doing a jump-stop, then swinging one leg back in a 180-degree turn so that you are facing back down court.

Faking. Dribbling around your defender or getting open for the shot often require that you force your defensive man off balance. A dip of the shoulders can deceive your defender and cause him to shift his weight in one direction while you drive past him in the other direction. A good head fake can get your defender to leave his feet, giving you the option to drive or to go up for the shot while he is on the way down.

Faking requires you to be an actor. Your advantage as an offensive player is that you know what you want to do, but your defender does not know your next move; he can only react to your movement. Therefore, you can play on his uncertainty by disguising your moves with a preliminary fake to get him to shift his balance and give you the edge. Nodding your head, shifting your weight, or looking one way and passing another can give you the instant you need to blow by your man.

Defensive Slide. The purpose of this drill is to become good at lateral movement without crossing your feet. Think of yourself as a cat as you move back and forth between two points on the floor— from one side of the lane to the other will do for starters. Twenty-eight or more times in 30 seconds is excellent.

Pump Fake. To get your defensive man off balance and to give yourself the opportunity to shoot, fake jumping up for a shot by raising your head and shoulders quickly, imitating the beginning of your shooting motion. If you are deceptive

Fundamentals

Defensive slide.

enough, your defender will leave his feet to block your shot. Wait until he is on the way down before you go up and you should have an open shot at the basket. Remember, your defender cannot read your mind and only can guess what you are going to do by watching your body movements.

Pump Fake 1.

Pump Fake 2.

Pump Fake 3.

Fundamentals

BASIC DRILLS

Transition. Starting low at the foul line, run hard to the baseline and then race backwards to the foul line again. Repeat. Twenty times or more in 30 seconds is excellent.

Lateral Dash. Starting at the top of the key, face courtside and slide laterally to the foul line. Push off from there with the outside leg back to the key. Repeat, always pushing off with the outside leg. Great for lateral movement. Thirty-five or more in 30 seconds is excellent.

X-Up. Start at the upper right-hand corner of the lane. Dribbling right-handed, drive to the right side of the basket for a right-handed layup. Rebound and dribble right-handed to the left corner of the basket. From there, use the left hand to dribble and drive the layup. Dribbling left-handed, cross to the right side of the lane and repeat. For excellence, set your goal at scoring 7 or more in 30 seconds.

Box Jump. Mark off four boxes in a rectangle on the floor. Then jump, feet together, over the lines into each box. Repeat. Eighty times in 60 seconds is excellent.

Basketball Jump.

Line Jump.

Jumping Rope. There's no greater exercise for improving agility than the old basic jumping rope. It provides excellent training for foot mobility. And moving the feet is the essence of basketball. An excellent performance is jumping 140 or more times per minute; 125 or more is good, and 100 or more is fair. Set a goal and attack it with gusto, taking time each day to work the ropes.

Basketball Jump. This drill is excellent for building knee and ankle quickness and strength. Jumping over the basketball 55 times or more in 30 seconds is excellent.

Line Jump. Pick a line on the court. Jump over it and jump back. One hundred twenty jumps in 30 seconds is excellent, 105 or better is good, and 90 is fair.

Screaming Eagle Jump. Develop your jumping ability and get out your frustrations with the spread-legged jump. Jump as high as you can, keeping your arms and legs straight. Not only will you jump better but you'll feel better. Do it 20 times in 30 seconds if you can.

Step Test. With a teammate holding the back of the chair, step up and down from the seat as quickly as you can. Twenty-five times in 30 seconds is excellent.

Screaming Eagle.

Step Test.

Double Ball Toss. Develop the use of your left hand by tossing a ball to your teammate on the other side of the lane using only your left hand. To make it interesting, use two balls and throw them at the same time.

Mikan Drill. This is a series of high-speed soft hooks up close. Shoot a right hander, rebound, and go to your left. Repeat the alternating shots as quickly and accurately as you can in 30 seconds. Excellent is 20 or more. Set goals and keep improving.

Mikan Drill 1.

Double Ball Toss.

Mikan Drill 2.

DEPTH JUMPS

Gary Colson
University of New Mexico

Several years ago I watched the U.S. Olympic volleyball team training program at Pepperdine University. I was amazed at the vertical jumping ability of each player. They all seemed to be jumping over 40 inches. Marv Dunphy, then coach of the U.S. and Pepperdine volleyball teams, told me that a member of the Cuban Olympic team could jump over 50 inches and that the Cuban team vertical jump average was 43 inches. Inquiring further, I learned that a lot of the team were using depth jumping to increase their jumping ability.

Needed for the drill are a mat (to protect the knees) and two boxes built of half-inch plywood. One box is to be 32 inches high; the other, 43 inches. Both should measure 18 inches square on each end.

Diagrams 1-8. Jumping from the lower box, land with both feet on the mat and immediately jump as high as you can. Taller players should carry a volleyball or basketball and dunk it on each jump. Repeat 20 times. Then repeat the same experience from the higher box. Do the exercise twice a week for a total of 80 jumps per week.

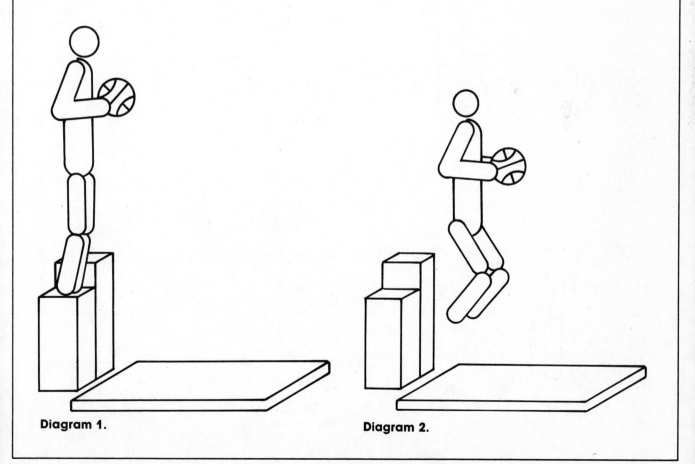

Diagram 1.

Diagram 2.

Fundamentals

Diagram 3.

Diagram 4.

Diagram 5.

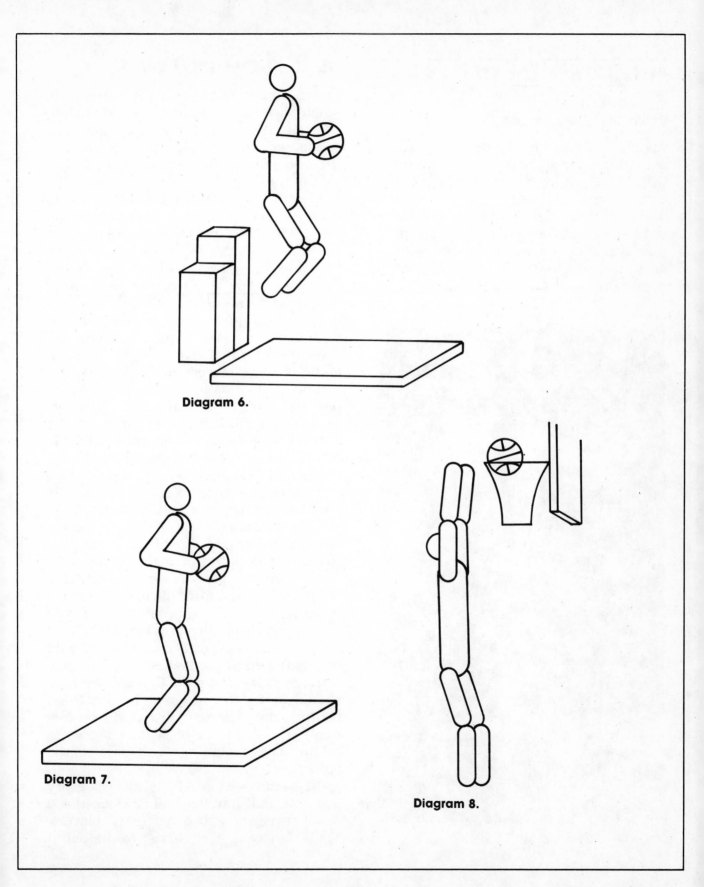

Diagram 6.

Diagram 7.

Diagram 8.

Fundamentals

FUNDAMENTAL DRILLS

Bill Frieder
University of Michigan

An effective way for a basketball coach to teach his philosophy is to use breakdown drills that can be easily learned and executed. These drills can be used at any level and are flexible, allowing a coach to focus individual and team attention on a particular fundamental aspect of the game—good passing, aggressive rebounding, communication, etc.

Bill Frieder, University of Michigan.

DRILL 1—THE SHELL DRILL

The primary purpose of this drill is to teach players how to react to team defensive situations. It emphasizes four key fundamentals: jumping to the ball, bumping the cutter, stopping all splits, and taking the charge.

We run the shell drill every day—60 to 90 seconds on each drill in the early season, 30 to 45 seconds toward the end. You can make these drills competitive to help motivate the players. Divide the squad into three teams that rotate as each group finishes playing defense through all four drills. Allow just three possessions for each drill (a total of 12 possessions).

We incorporate three rules in our shell game to force players to concentrate: no dribbling is allowed in the jump-to-the-ball and bump-the-cutter drills; only two dribbles are allowed in the stop-the-splits and take-the-change drills; and the drills continue until a defensive rebound or a completed field goal.

Diagram 1—Jump to the Ball. Pass the ball around the perimeter; each player should initially hold it for two counts. Defensive players should move on the flight of the ball and react before their man receives a pass. Player X1 guarding the passer should force his man to make a basket cut behind him, taking away the return pass from the wing. Players X3 and X4, two passes away from the ball, should be positioned in the lane.

Diagram 2—Bump the Cutter. Player X1 should bump the cutter so he has to go behind him. Players X3 and X4 on the weak side should be alert for chances to bump players making flash cuts to the ball.

Diagram 3—Stop All Splits. On every pass the ball handler will dribble into a gap between the two defensive players. The defensive player closest to the ball—

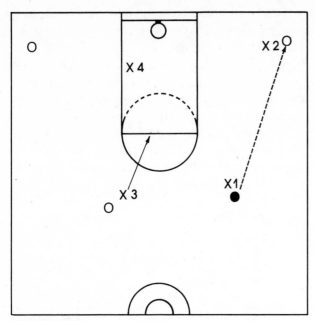

Diagram 1.

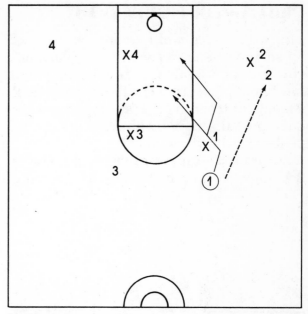

Diagram 2.

X1—should pinch down to stop penetration, thus preventing the offense from splitting the two defensive players. Players X3 and X4 should rotate and communicate with their teammates trying to prevent the split.

Diagram 4—Take the Charge. Player X2

misses a steal attempt, resulting in his man driving hard to the basket. Player X4 must move into position to change the direction of the ball or take the charge. Other players must be alert for rotation responsibilities to prevent passes to the baseline and the free throw area.

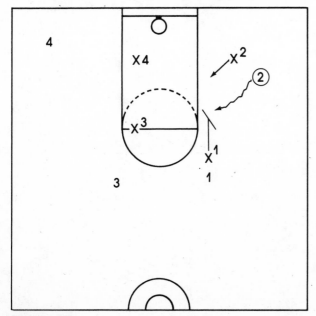

Diagram 3.

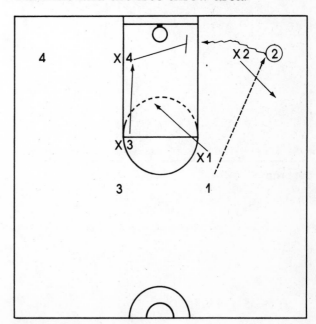

Diagram 4.

Fundamentals

DRILL 2—THE FIGURE EIGHT

This drill serves multiple purposes on defense and offense. Players must make accurate passes against pressure and make hard and quick cuts. The figure-eight drill is good for teaching the jab step on basket cuts, post-up moves, and feeding the low post from the wing.

Diagram 5—Figure-Eight Entry. Player 2 makes an up-and-out cut to the wing and takes a pass from 1, who makes a cut to the basket. Player 3 makes a jab step at the basket and replaces the cutter. Player 2 looks for a quick pass to the cutter on the low post. The defense should concentrate on preventing 1 from passing, cutting, or even dribbling.

Diagram 6—Figure-Eight Reset. Player 2 passes back to 3 and moves to the opposite top. The drill resumes with 1 making the up-and-out cut.

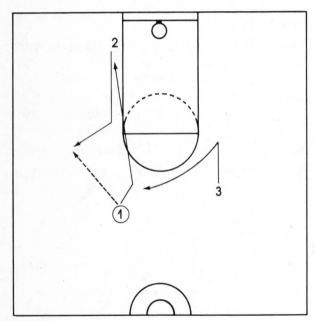

Diagram 5.

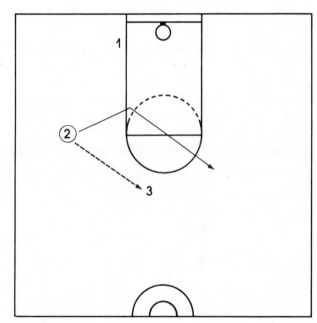

Diagram 6.

DRILL 3—STATION WORK

Station work is used for conditioning and to improve individual skills. The drills in each station are done 15 times at the start and are increased to 30, four days a week. There are seven stations: rim touches; left-handed tips; right-handed tips; power pick-ups (big men must dunk); ante-over rebounding; left and right baseline shooting; and free throw shooting. After the drills players run one-on-one sprints.

DRILL 4—FAST-BREAK DRILLS

We use several drills for teaching fast-break situations. Again, each drill teaches offensive and defensive reactions. In a three-on-two fast break, players running the outside lanes should make a 45-degree cut toward the basket at the foul line extended. In a two-on-one situation, the ball handler should attack the basket and make the defender commit to the ball or the open man, who should position himself about a step behind the ball line to create an angle for the drop-off pass.

In all fast-break situations, the ball handler should slow his pace as he nears the scoring area; he must be under control to make the play—pass, short jumper, or layup. Players waiting for a pass should have their hands up.

Diagram 7—Weave/Two-on-One Back. Players 1, 2, and 3 run the weave to the opposite end. The player who scores or causes the turnover becomes the defensive player and must sprint to the top of the key to prevent the other two players from scoring.

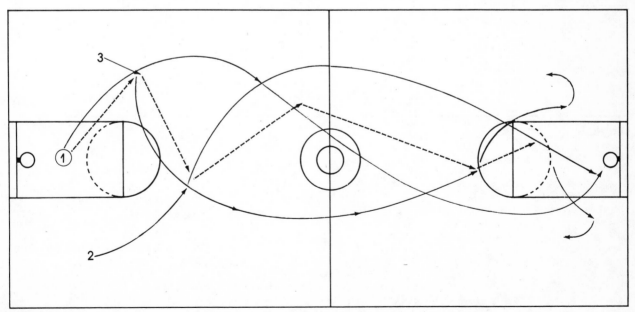

Diagram 7.

Three-on-Two/Two-on-One. Two defensive players set up in tandem at the top of the key and the dotted line in the lane. Three offensive players attack, and the player who shoots or causes the turnover must retreat on defense while the two defensive players convert to offense. The two leftover players remain at the basket in order to play defense against the next group.

Diagram 8—Three-on-Two with Chaser. Players 1, 2, 3, X1, and X2 run a regular three-on-two drill. Player X3, on the sideline at half court, sprints to the center circle; he must touch the inner circle before joining the defense under the basket.

Two defensive players are waiting at the other end and a third is at half court. At the change of possession, the first defensive trio converts to offense.

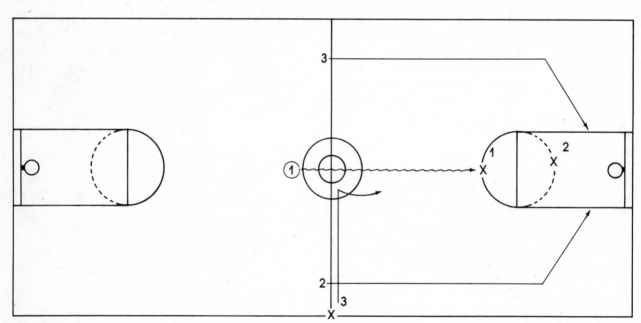

Diagram 8.

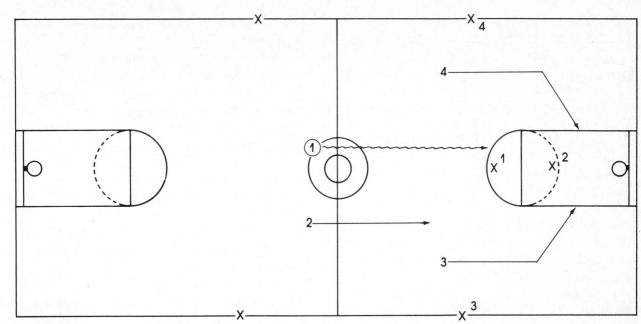

Diagram 9.

Diagram 9—Four-on-Two with Chasers. Add a fourth offensive player and two defensive players stationed at the 28-foot marks on either side. When the ball crosses an imaginary line between the marks, each player sprints toward the lane to pick up a man.

Diagram 10—Three-on-Three Fast Break. Player 1 will attack either elbow of the lane. In this case 2, on the ball side, screens for 3 in the lane. Player 1 attempts a pass to 3 and sets a diagonal down-screen for 2; 3 can shoot or pass to 2 cutting to the foul line area.

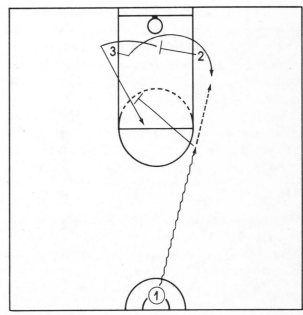

Diagram 10.

The best ball handler should have the ball on a three-on-three fast break, and he should take it to the middle of the court so he can go to either elbow. He should keep dribbling until he is ready to pass. The screener should be alert for defensive switches and pin his man or step back to the ball. If he doesn't get the ball, he should continue to the opposite box. Players who will be cutting off screens should jab-step in the direction their man is playing them before making their cut.

Fundamentals

REFLECTIONS

John Wooden
UCLA (retired)

Two things I always wanted in players were balance and controlled quickness. This was true when I was a high school coach, it never changed when I moved to the college level, and it would not change today even if I were coaching professionals.

I wanted quickness. Did I want size? Of course I did, but unlike some of my peers, I would sacrifice some size for speed and quickness.

I believe the most important thing in basketball, just as in life, is balance. You must keep things in perspective. Think of the balance you must have in playing the game—physical balance, team balance, rebounding balance, court balance, squad balance.

I began practice every day with drills for physical balance. We started with feet as wide as the shoulders, head at mid-point above the feet, chin up so vision is not impaired, hands in front and close to the body, and joints flexed and relaxed.

Drill 1. Loosen up individually for two minutes. Stretch, squat, twist—move every joint.

Drill 2. Jump shot. Concentrate on proper form and balance.

Drill 3. Freeze the defense and shoot. Use body and head fakes—no ball fakes.

Drill 4. Go by the defense. Raise defensive man by fake and go by him, not around him.

Drill 5. Jump ball. Hands at shoulder level; explode with jump.

Drill 6. Offensive rebounding. Hands above shoulders and palms forward.

A. Work on tipping the ball on a missed rebound.

B. Bring the ball down close to the chest, make one pump fake, and go back up for the shot.

Drill 7. Defensive rebounding.

A. Use crossover step on reverse pivot to get in path of offensive man. Don't block out—go hard for strong rebound.

B. Work on outlet pass.

Drill 8. Change of direction.

Drill 9. Change of pace to mid-court, defensive sliding back to line.

Drill 10. Repeat drills 8 and 9 in pairs and reverse at mid-court.

Drill 11. One-on-one dribbling and defense—no dribbling behind the back or through the legs.

These are basketball drills as well as conditioning drills. I always worked on balance and technique. I don't believe in running solely for conditioning, but I do favor short sprints repeated frequently.

Now here is what I think was the best drill I used. I liked to run it for ten minutes each practice; and, except for the day before a game, hardly a day went by that we didn't run this drill. In my book this was a conditioning drill.

Diagram 1. The defense—11 and 12—starts out on the top of the circle and medium post. Player 2 puts the ball on the board, gets the rebound, and starts down the middle of the floor. He may make one pass to 2 or 3 on either side, but the ball must be back in the middle by mid-court. When the ball is halfway between the two circles, trailer 10 enters into the defense. The offense should only have time for one or two passes before shooting.

Diagram 2. As the shot is taken, 4 and 5 move to the outer circle and retreat to their defensive positions. Players 10, 11, and 12 rebound the shot and bring the ball back on offense. Player 6 enters as defensive trailer. Players 1, 2, and 3 return to their respective lines.

We ran the drill this way the first week. In the second week the last offense player to touch the ball played defense to mid-court after the rebound. And in the third week all three offensive men played defense back to mid-court. This is a very good drill for the transition from offense to defense.

I favored the high-post offensive because it gives a team good rebounding position and gives each player an equal opportunity to score.

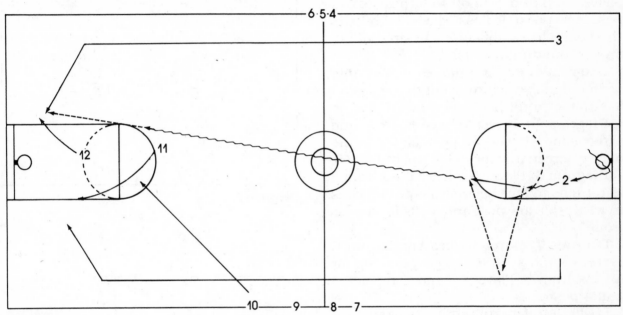

Diagram 1.

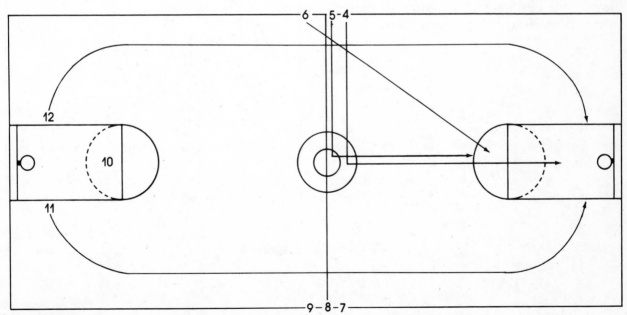

Diagram 2.

HIGH-POST DRILLS

Diagram 3. Player 2 penetrates a couple of dribbles and passes to 1. This passing angle should keep the defense from intercepting the pass. Player 1 first looks for 5 cutting into the high-post area. Player 1 passes to 3 and cuts off high post to low post for a possible pass. Player 4 moves to the board to establish the desired offensive rebounding triangle.

Diagram 4. Player 3 passes to 5 in high post and makes a strong cut to the basket looking for a return pass.

Diagram 5. Player 3 passes to 5 and screens for 1 in the low post. Player 1 cuts off the screen and looks for a pass from 5.

Diagram 6. Player 5 takes a pass from 3 and turns to face defense. Player 4 moves to weak-side low post and looks for a pass from 5.

Diagram 7. Player 5 takes a pass from 1. Players 3 and 4 cut to low post looking for a pass from 5. Players 1 and 2 replace 3 and 4 positions.

I believe in few rules but lots of suggestions. I tried to do a good job of preparing players for games; performance in games depends on how well you practice.

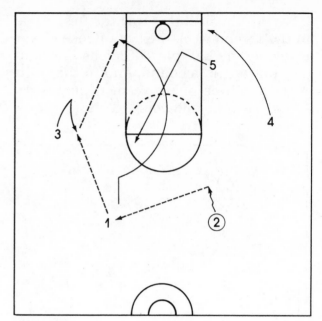

Diagram 3.

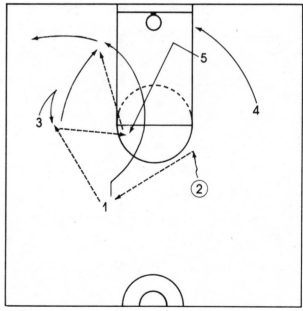

Diagram 4.

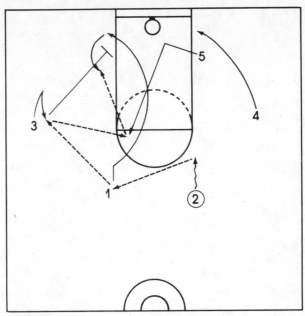

Diagram 5.

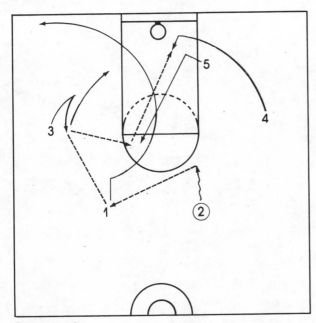

Diagram 6.

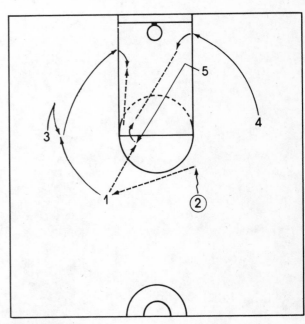

Diagram 7.

Fundamentals

Oliver Robinson, University of Alabama-Birmingham.

4
SHOOTING

While proficiency in all the fundamental skills of basketball—dribbling, passing, rebounding, defense, and shooting—is necessary for playing winning basketball, shooting may be the most important. Well-executed passes and efficient dribbling can set up high-percentage shots, but the ball must still be tossed through the hoop to light up the scoreboard.

A variety of shots are available to the player: the jump shot, the layup, the set shot, and the hook. Many of the game's greatest shooters—Bill Sharman, Pete Maravich, Larry Bird—have combined hard work and dedication with their natural athletic abilities to become preeminent scorers. Shooting, like the other fundamentals, is a skill that can be learned and perfected with practice.

Good shooting demands accuracy. Achieving accuracy requires good technique, good shot selection, and confidence that you can make the shot. While there is

no *right* way to shoot a basketball, the beginning player or the player trying to find his style can improve his shooting by keeping certain fundamentals in mind. What is important is that you feel comfortable and confident when attempting the shot.

You must have good balance when you are shooting. Distribute your weight on both feet so that you feel comfortable. For the set shot, as in shooting free throws, many players use a boxer's stance, placing one foot slightly in front of the other. Other players keep their feet parallel. In any case, your feet should be about shoulders' width apart. A right-handed shooter in the boxer's stance will have the right foot slightly forward; a left-handed shooter, the left foot. The legs should be flexed because the power behind your shot comes more from the spring in your legs than from the thrusting of your arm. When you release the ball, rock forward on the balls of your feet and shift your weight forward to your toes.

When you shoot the jump shot, remember to jump straight up without falling to either side. Going straight up allows you to line up your shot directly with the rim of the basket. Moving sideways while you attempt the shot just means that your eyes and brain must do a lot more calculating to tell your muscles how to aim the ball. In other words, square your body with the basket, and then all your brain will have to do is calculate the distance to the rim.

Releasing the ball with a fluid, soft touch will increase your chances of making your shot. Grip the ball lightly with your fingers spread evenly around the ball. Leave a small space between the ball and the palm of the hand. Just as you don't want to shoot flat-footed and diminish your balance, you do not want to palm the ball and lessen your feel for it.

To line up the shot, make sure your elbow is directly under the basketball and in line with the basket. Beginners often let their elbows project out from their bodies, which complicates their aim. As you raise your arm to shoot, your elbow should be pointing toward the basket. Shoot by extending your arm and snapping the wrist forward. Your fingers should be pointing at the basket during the follow-through.

When you shoot, your body should uncoil like a spring. The shot begins in the feet, and the motion extends smoothly through the legs, the torso, and the arms. Remember, the power for your shot comes from your legs; the arms and wrist are used mainly to guide the ball. Above all, the key to developing an accurate shot is to find a shooting motion that feels natural and comfortable.

A word about follow-through: Just as a golfer continues his swing well past the point of contact with the ball, a basketball player should continue the forward motion of his arm past the point where the ball is released. Continue the motion as if you are trying to stick your arm right into the basket.

Most good shooters release the ball with a slight backspin. When you put a slight spin on the ball, you tend to loft your shot more softly and with a higher arc. As a rule, try to put about a 45-degree arc on the ball so the shot approaches the rim from above, which gives it more of the rim's diameter to fall through. The diameter of the basket is twice the diameter of the ball, so two balls can fall through the basket at the same time if they are dropped from directly above the rim. Lofting the ball so that it enters the basket from above gives you a larger target area.

Aim the ball at either the front or at the back of the rim. Keep your eye on the rim as you shoot and resist the temptation to follow the motion of the ball toward the basket. If you raise your head to follow the ball, you will break the concentration you need to aim the ball and you will not follow through properly.

Of course, being a good shooter takes more than understanding good technique. You must be in condition both physically and mentally to carry out what you have learned. Top physical conditioning will enable your muscles to carry out your intentions, and mental toughness will give you the confidence and courage to do your best.

Just as you can enhance your physical skills, you can build your confidence. The first step in building confidence is to hone your skills to the point where you feel comfortable. Larry Bird frequently practices his shot for two hours before a game. If Larry feels he needs the practice, then it's a sure bet you do. It might also help if you visualize your shot going in and think about making your shot instead of missing it. Of course, even good shooters will miss more shots than they make, so keeping up confidence is a continuous struggle, even for accomplished players.

Johnny Dawkins (left), Duke University.

One other important aspect of good shooting is knowing when to take the shot—good shot selection. Taking the right shot at the right time will increase your field-goal accuracy and help you keep friends on the court and in the stands. Every player from the NBA to the church leagues has contended with players who will ignore a teammate standing wide open under the basket and launch one into the stratosphere. When you put up a wild shot that bounces off the rim, your team misses a scoring opportunity and you lose a few more votes for the all-star team. Know your range, and remember to take the shots that are most successful for you. Just as a five-foot guard should not try to stuff one in your face, neither should the player with wooden hands try a three-pointer. Get yourself into position to take the shots you know you can make. After you release your shot, follow the ball to the basket for a rebound or be ready to get back on defense.

SET SHOT

Until it was replaced by the jump shot, the set shot was the preeminent shot in basketball. It was popularized by a great Stanford University player in the 1930s, Hank Luisetti. When the one-handed set shot replaced the two-handed set shot, it was considered one of the most far-reaching innovations in the game. Although the one-handed set shot has been mostly replaced by the jump shot, it is still used at the free throw line. And some players, most notably Larry Bird, use it from the field because the stance allows the player to do a number of things besides shoot the ball. From the set shot stance, you are in good position to make a pass toward the basket or to drive around your defender for a layup. By not jumping to take the

Shooting

shot, you do not commit yourself to one course of action and can keep your defender off balance.

Becoming proficient at the set shot is a matter of practice. The "around-the-world" drill is effective: shoot the ball from different positions on the court 15–20 feet from the basket. Also try the shot under game conditions, when you have a hand in your face and are physically tired. However, before you toughen the shooting conditions, practice the shot enough by yourself in order to feel comfortable with it.

Establish your shooting range by practicing the shot from different distances from the basket. When you are shooting alone, you should be able to make 60 percent of your shots from a particular spot in order to consider yourself proficient from that range. If you can't hit 60 percent, you should consider decreasing your range.

To shoot the set shot:

- hold the ball firmly in both hands and face the basket.
- balance your weight evenly on both feet, with the foot on the side of your shooting arm advanced slightly ahead of the other foot.

Set Shot 2.

- flex your legs and use the spring in your legs to get the power into your shot; hold the ball just above shoulder height or slightly to the side of your face and aim for the rim of the basket; remember to follow through with your wrist when you release the ball.

Set Shot 1.

Set Shot 3.

JUMP SHOT

Just as the one-hand set shot replaced the two-hand set shot in the 1930s, the jump shot replaced the one-handed set shot in the 1950s. Unlike the set shot, the jump shot is usually made on the move. It allows you to shoot over an opponent's outstretched arms and can be executed very quickly.

When you take a jump shot, you should release the ball at the height of your jump. At that moment, your body will be nearly stationary, and you will not have to compensate for the momentum of your body when you shoot. Because you are often moving prior to the shot, it is important to plant your inside foot, the foot toward the basket, firmly when you stop your dribble or receive a pass. Flex your legs and spring into the air, remembering to square your shoulders with the basket.

Variations of the jump shot include the fall-away jumper and the bank shot. The fall-away shot is difficult because it is shot off balance. However, it enables you to shoot over a much taller player by creating the extra space necessary to get off the shot. The bank shot is a jump shot aimed at the backboard instead of the rim. The bank shot is also useful when you are approaching the basket at high speed and are out of control. Banking the ball softens the shot, making it a wiser choice than a jump shot aimed directly at the rim.

To shoot the jump shot:

- plant your inside foot firmly as you turn toward the basket.
- square-up your shoulders toward the basket; keep the elbow straight and pointed toward the basket.
- shoot the ball at the height of your jump and follow through.

Jump Shot 1.

Jump Shot 2.

Jump Shot 3.

Jump Shot 4.

Jump Shot 5.

Shooting

LAYUP

The layup is the highest percentage shot in basketball with the exception of the slam-dunk. It is the shot you are working for when you start the fast break or when you pass the ball quickly around the court in a half-court offense. You don't really shoot a layup, but you do as its name suggests: lay up the ball against the backboard near the basket.

As you drive toward the basket, spring off the foot opposite your shooting arm. Carry the ball up with both hands to secure it from defenders. When you release the ball, the palm of your hand should be facing the basket. Don't snap your wrist forward as you would for the jump shot or set shot; the momentum of your body will carry the ball toward the rim. But don't let your momentum carry your body too far under the basket. Think of yourself as a high jumper rather than a broad jumper. You might consider laying the ball up underhanded to further soften the impact with the backboard.

A large part of feeling comfortable shooting the layup is feeling comfortable dribbling. You have to make it to the basket with the ball in your hands. When you are out of control, the ball often ends up bouncing off your knee and into the stands. It is important that you be able to dribble without looking at the ball because you need to concentrate on moving around your defender and eyeing the rim.

If you are approaching the basket from the front rather than the side, it is probably easier to lay the ball up over the rim without using the backboard. Jump up just as you do for regular layups and don't let your momentum carry you too far under the basket.

To be a complete basketball player, you must learn to use both hands equally well.

Layup.

You must be able to shoot a layup with either hand.

To shoot a layup:

- get your dribble under control and move as quickly as you can toward the basket.
- jump off the foot opposite your shooting arm.
- jump as high as you can and bounce the ball off the backboard.

HOOK

The hook shot is considered the exclusive property of centers who use it to loft the ball over opposing seven-footers. However, a variation of the sweeping hook is used by forwards and guards when they are close to the basket and need to shoot over taller opposition. The hook shot keeps the ball farther away from the defender. It serves the same purpose as the fall-away jumper: it keeps you from eating three pounds of basketball leather.

The sweeping hook is a difficult shot. You begin the shooting motion with your back to the basket. Good balance is essential, because you will be pivoting on the foot opposite your shooting hand. If you are shooting a right-handed hook, you will raise your right leg almost parallel to the floor at the same time that you raise your arm to shoot. As soon as you begin to pivot, turn your head and look back over your shoulder to sight the basket. To line up your shot, imagine a straight line extending from your shooting arm through both your shoulders to the rim. Raise your arm with a fluid motion and snap your wrist to release the ball at the point when your arm reaches its greatest extension above your head. Your fingers should point toward the rim during your follow-through.

A variation of the hook is the hook layup. It is particularly useful to smaller players as they drive the lane and have to launch the ball over much taller opponents. Improvisation is often the rule when you drive through the tall timber, but the basic technique for the hook layup is the same as for the regular hook, except that you will shoot it on the run rather than from a stationary position.

To shoot the hook:

- hold the ball firmly about chest high.
- pivot toward the basket on your inside foot, the foot opposite your shooting hand.
- turn your head and sight the basket or backboard.
- raise your arm with a fluid motion and release the ball with a snap of your wrist at the highest point above your head.
- follow through with your fingers pointing toward the basket.

Hook Shot.

Shooting

DUNK

Oh, what a feeling! To jam the ball through the cords and slam it off the floor! The crowd goes crazy and the adrenaline rushes through your body as you race back down court. The dunk is an exciting play, and it can change the tempo of the game and give your team and your fans a boost in morale.

And it is a high-percentage shot, provided you can jump high enough to get the ball over the rim. We church leaguers know the embarrassment of sweeping in for the dunk only to have our tired legs fail us: we rise only nine-and-a-half feet into the air and wedge the ball between our hand and the front of the rim. If you are going to hot-dog it, be sure that you can pull it off. It's hard to hide on a basketball court.

Every player who can dunk has his own style. What you need to dunk is the ability to jump high and to be strong enough to carry the ball up to the rim in the midst of a crowd of defenders. Once you have the ball over the rim, snap your wrist to thrust the ball forcefully through the net.

For a time the dunk was banished from the list of legal shots because it requires your putting your hand in the imaginary cylinder above the rim. You cannot touch the ball while it is rolling around the rim or while it is in the area that extends above the rim. The shot was banned for several years in college and high school competition. But the dunk is back, and "Spud" Webb, 5'4", has shown emphatically that it is not just for the big men.

Dunk 1.

Dunk 2.

Dunk 3.

Dunk 4.

Shooting

Lazy Man's Shooting Drill. By lying flat on your back and softly tossing the ball straight up, you will develop a soft release and learn to shoot using a flick of your wrist. Repeat until you misfire and catch the ball on your nose!

Lazy Man's Drill 1.

Lazy Man's Drill 2.

Lazy Man's Drill 3.

Shooting

Hurry-Up Shooting Drill. Place two balls on the court, one on either side of the lane. Shoot one ball, retrieve it, and place it back on the side of the lane. Run to the other side of the lane and pick up the second ball and shoot. Retrieve the second ball and place it on the floor again. Alternate shooting and following your shot from each side of the lane; do this as many times as you can in 60 seconds.

Hurry-Up Drill 1.

Hurry-Up Drill 2.

Hurry-Up Drill 3.

Hurry-Up Drill 4.

Shooting

Steve Mitchell (with ball), University of Alabama-Birmingham.

5
PASSING, DRIBBLING, AND REBOUNDING

PASSING

A sizzling pass that catches the defense off guard and sets up your teammate for an easy layup is a coach's delight and can make you feel as good as sinking a shot from 25 feet. Crisp, precise passing can lead to easy baskets and keep the defense a step behind. Whether you are fast-breaking or whipping the ball around the key in your half-court offense, passing is the quickest way to move the ball and the most efficient way to get the highest-percentage shots.

Becoming an effective passer involves more than just learning the techniques. You must have good court vision and be able to anticipate the movement of your teammates, and, of course, you must not reveal your intention to pass by "telegraphing." Good passers give up the ball to a teammate unselfishly; they take pride in their passes. The pass should be another tool in your offensive arsenal and not just a way to get rid of the ball because you don't know what to do with it. As in every aspect of basketball, you must think ahead.

When you pass, control the ball with your fingertips and snap your wrists on your release to give it some zip. Making lazy passes will result in turnovers and lost scoring opportunities for your team.

Let's take a look at the variety of passes you can use to outmaneuver your defender.

The **chest pass** is thrown by bringing the basketball chest high and gripping it tightly with thumbs and middle fingers. Release the ball with a snap of the wrists and extend your elbows, giving the ball backspin and sending it on a line-drive trajectory. After you release the ball, your palms should face the receiver and your thumbs should point down. While you are learning the pass, step toward the receiver with whatever foot feels natural to improve your aim and give the ball a little extra speed.

The chest pass is generally used in situations where there is no defender between you and the receiver—moving the ball around the perimeter of the defense or bringing the ball up court, for example. It is an efficient pass that can be thrown with accuracy.

The technique for throwing the two-handed **bounce pass** is the same as for the chest pass, except that it is delivered with a bounce. It is often used to get the ball to the post position or to teammates cutting to the basket. The ball should bounce

Chest Pass 1.

Chest Pass 2.

about two-thirds of the way to the receiver so that he can catch it about waist high. The bounce pass can also be made directly off the dribble by using one hand to push the ball toward the receiver.

Although the bounce pass is relatively slow, it is difficult to intercept and should be used when you're passing in traffic.

The **overhead pass** is becoming increasingly popular as a way to throw the ball over zone defenses and to feed the ball to big men in the post. The ball is held above the head with both hands and is thrown with a snap of the wrists. After you throw the ball, your palms should end up facing the floor while your fingers point in the direction of the receiver.

Chest Pass 3.

As its name suggests, the **baseball pass** is thrown the same way you throw a baseball. The ball is brought behind the head with one hand and released like a right fielder's throw to home plate. It is used for long passes up court when you need to cover a long distance quickly, like when you make a long outlet pass after a defensive rebound or when you take the ball out of bounds under your opponent's basket.

The biggest problem in throwing the baseball pass is its tendency to curve if you throw it with too much side-armed motion. It is very important to throw it with a straight overhead motion so that the ball will travel in a straight line to your teammate. Try not to throw the pass too high because a defender will have more time to intercept it. Put some steam behind your pass.

The **hook pass** is useful when you are being closely guarded. By stepping to the side of your defender, you can pass around him using a sweeping motion of the arm. The hook pass is often used to get the ball inside to the pivot.

The **lob** is a variation of the overhead pass used to get the ball into the center or low post. It is primarily made to taller players who can outreach defenders for the ball. It is usually made two-handed and is thrown with a very high arc. A lob from a perimeter passer to a high-leaping inside player can set up the slam dunk if the players time the pass precisely. A timely lob pass high over the rim to a Michael Jordan or a Ralph Sampson can be an effective scoring weapon.

The **behind-the-back pass** is a higher-risk pass that should be used only when you cannot use a safer pass like the bounce pass or chest pass. As you bring your hand behind your back to make the pass, shift your body slightly forward to gain clearance for the ball. Release the ball with a flick of your wrist. Use this pass primarily when you are boxed in by a defender.

Receiving passes requires concentration and constant movement to try to get open. When you are receiving a pass, move to meet the ball in order to prevent your defender from deflecting or stealing it. Catch the ball on your fingertips and with good balance, so you will be ready to continue the play with another pass, a dribble, or a shot. Protect the ball from your defender by shielding him from the ball with your body.

To be an effective passer:

- be alert to the movement of players and know when your pass can be completed.

- don't telegraph your passes.
- think ahead; after you pass the ball, be ready to move to continue the play.
- give your teammates crisp, accurate passes.

Two-Ball Passing Drill. With a teammate, run the length of the court passing two balls back and forth. One player should use the chest pass; the other, a bounce pass. This drill will help develop hand-eye coordination.

Wall Toss. Using the chest pass and the bounce pass, toss the ball off the wall and get in position to catch the rebound. The closer you move to the wall, the bigger the test for your reflexes.

Two-Ball Passing Drill 1.

Two-Ball Passing Drill 2.

Wall Ball Toss.

DRIBBLING

Every coach will tell you the same thing: "Learn to dribble without watching the ball. Keep your head up and watch where you're going." That's good advice. But what about those of us who have a hard time dribbling even when we watch the ball?

I know a player who can make free throws with his eyes closed. But he learned with his eyes open. So when you are learning to dribble, it's all right to watch the ball until you get a feel for how the ball bounces. Dribbling is also the first skill in basketball that you will want to master with both hands. You may get by without being able to shoot with both hands, but there is no way you'll make it dribbling with only one hand.

Dribbling needs to become second nature to you. Many beginning basketball players take a basketball with them everywhere they go. The secret to becoming a good dribbler is to dribble a lot.

Good dribbling enables you to penetrate the defense or to set up a teammate. You can control the tempo of the game with the dribble, slowing the pace with a walk dribble or picking up the tempo with a fast-break dribble.

Crouch when you dribble, in order to keep the ball low; the lower the bounce, the less chance for a defender to steal it from you. Control the ball with your fingertips, not with the palm of your hand. Don't slap the ball to the floor—push it to the floor, keeping your hand in contact with the ball as long as possible. Keep your head up so you will be alert to the action on the floor.

Dribbling on the fast break requires that you push the ball out in front of you and run to catch up to it. Of course, you will not crouch when you're dribbling on the break.

The crossover dribble, changing hands with the basketball, is necessary when you change directions. Just before you switch hands, lower the height of the dribble and quickly push it to your opposite hand.

The reverse dribble is a good way to change directions when you are stopped by a defender. Unlike the crossover dribble, where you continue to face the defender when you change hands, the reverse dribble is executed by turning away from your defender and switching the ball to your other hand while you pivot. It can be a very effective means of confusing your defender because you can reverse first in one direction and then the other.

The behind-the-back dribble is for experts only. It is used to change direction or to elude a defender when you are being guarded closely and cannot safely use a crossover dribble. Move the ball behind your back and push it with a low bounce to the opposite hand. Be sure to keep your feet out of the way or what was meant to be a flashy maneuver may cause you to lose the ball.

Some other points to remember: Don't get carried away with dribbling and forget about the rest of the team. Be careful not to pick up your dribble coming up court and allow yourself to be double-teamed. Keep your dribble alive until you know what your next move will be. Always keep your body and your free arm between you and the defender to help protect the ball.

To be an effective dribbler:

- stay in a crouch and keep the ball low.
- control the ball with your fingertips.
- practice, practice, practice.

REBOUNDING

Rebounding is not for the timid or faint of heart. You don't need to think like Genghis Khan to be a good rebounder, but if you are put off by the swarms of shoppers who surround Macy's sales tables after Christmas, you need to work on mental toughness. Rebounding is hard manual labor—the kind that will get you a few bumps and bruises. Rebounding demands hustle and determination. It is competitive—you have to want the ball more than the other guys. It is unselfish—you do it to help the team. Good rebounders are the type of guys who will play catcher on the baseball team or nose guard on the football team if it means a chance to compete.

Coaches keep the score in rebounds just as they keep the score in baskets made. Rebounds on the offensive end of the court will give your team second, third, or fourth chances to score, and rebounds on the defensive end will prevent your opponent from getting those second-chance hoops.

Anticipate that each shot will be missed. When the shooter releases the ball, follow its flight and try to determine if the shot will be long, short, or off to the side. Communicate with your teammates so they will know what to expect.

Move into position for the rebound and block your opponent off the boards by keeping your body between him and the basket. Use a reverse pivot to face the basket and spread your arms and legs to claim more room under the basket. Keep your knees bent to maintain proper balance. Blocking out is the first step in gaining the rebounding advantage.

When the ball comes off the boards, time your jump and go up strong. Grasp the ball firmly with both hands and pull it toward your body. Protect the ball jealously. After all, you've worked to get it. Without being flagrant, you can help protect the ball by extending your elbows. Swinging the elbows vigorously is unsportsmanlike, can cause serious injury, and will result in a foul.

When you pull down a defensive rebound, look immediately for the outlet pass to start the fast break. Don't hold the ball or get trapped by a defensive double-team. If an outlet man is unavailable you may need to dribble out of traffic and start the fast break yourself.

When you rebound on the offensive end of the court, stay active and learn to judge how a missed shot will carom off the rim or backboard. As in defensive rebounding, remember to establish good rebounding position by blocking your opponent off the board. Often, however, the defender will have established inside position. In this case, either try to force the defender farther under the basket, or elude him when he turns toward the basket to block you out. Experienced players who are good leapers can tip a missed shot back toward the rim, but beginning players should grab the rebound with both hands and land before going back up with a stick-back. If your team does not get the rebound, fall back on defense.

To be a good rebounder:

- anticipate where the shot will come off the backboard.
- block your opponent off the board and establish good inside position.
- explode off the floor and go up strong for the rebound.
- when you grab the defensive rebound, look to make the outlet pass to start the fast break; on offense, try for the stick-back.

Blocking Out on the Rebound 1.

Blocking Out on the Rebound 2.

Blocking Out on the Rebound 3.

BALL-HANDLING DRILLS

Moving the basketball around the court quickly is one key to keeping the defense off balance. You must learn to handle the ball with speed and rhythm. The following drills can help.

Drill 1—Leg Circles. Starting in a semi-crouched position, legs apart, with the ball held in front of you at knee-level, circle one of your legs with the ball. Pass the ball from your right hand to your left hand. As you feel comfortable, increase the speed with which you move the ball.

Drill 2—Figure Eight. Again starting in a semi-crouched position, legs apart, carry the ball between your legs with your right hand and transfer it to your left hand as you bring the ball around your left leg. Continuing the same motion, pass the ball between your legs with your left hand and transfer it to your right hand as you circle your right leg.

Drill 3—Around Both Legs and the Body. Bend over slightly more than in the previous two drills and stand with your feet closer together. With the ball held in front of you, circle it first around your ankles and then around your knees. Starting with the ball in front of you, carry it around your back with your right hand, and then transfer it to your left hand as you bring it back around the front. Then, straighten up and pass the ball around your waist. Repeat the exercise by rotating the ball around your body in the opposite direction.

Figure Eight 1.

Figure Eight 2.

Drill 4—Dribble Through the Legs. Do this drill the same way you did Drill 2, but this time dribble the ball through your legs.

Drill 5—Fingertip Drill. To improve your ability to control the ball with your fingertips, stand straight and hold the ball in front of you with your arms straight and your elbows stiff. Tap the ball rapidly from one hand to the other as you move your arms from waist level to above your head.

Drill 6—Crab Run. As you run in a crouched position, pass the ball between your legs and exchange the ball from one hand to the other. Stay low and move the ball in a figure-eight pattern through your legs.

Dribble Through the Legs 1.

Dribble Through the Legs 2.

Dribble Through the Legs 3.

Fingertip Drill 1.

Fingertip Drill 2.

Fingertip Drill 3.

Crab Run.

Passing, Dribbling, and Rebounding

Drill 7—Dribble Through Legs. When proficient in the crab run, try the same drill dribbling the ball between your legs.

Combat Rebounding. When you rebound in the lane, you've got to be ready to take your lumps. With two other players, position yourself under the basket and take the ball back up. As you go up, your teammates will push you and hit your arms. Hold the ball tightly and go up strong and with determination to put the ball in the basket. This drill will help you go for the three-point play.

Two-Handed Rebounding. Rebound with two hands. To get you used to using both hands, tip the ball with one hand while you touch the backboard with the other hand.

Combat Rebounding 1.

Combat Rebounding 2.

Two-Handed Rebounding 1.

Two-Handed Rebounding 2.

Passing, Dribbling, and Rebounding

THE REBOUND GAME

Bill Leatherman
Bridgewater College

The Rebound Game is without a doubt the finest drill I have ever seen for teaching offensive and defensive rebounding. It is so tough and competitive that you will find it necessary to tone down your team's aggressiveness.

I believe that at one time or another every coach has asked himself, "What can I do to improve our rebounding?" There just don't seem to be as many rebounding drills to choose from as there are defensive drills, offensive drills, fast-break drills, etc. I have used this drill for all my nineteen seasons of coaching—thirteen years of high school and six at James Madison University. I can almost guarantee that it is the only rebounding drill you need to make your team "better off the glass."

RULES FOR THE THREE-ON-THREE REBOUND GAME

Divide your squad into four teams of three players each. If possible, each team should have a big man, a forward, and a guard. Use your managers as perimeter shooters (see diagram).

Team 1 is "under" first (defensive rebounders); they stay in that position for as long as they can maintain control of the rebound after each shot or are fouled by team 2.

Team 1 is credited with one point for each rebound cleared inbounds (see chart). The emphasis is on control of the ball in game situations. Team 1 stays until they do not control the rebound.

Team 2 (offensive team) can score in two ways: if they get an offensive rebound they get one point; if they score the offensive

Bill Leatherman (middle), Bridgewater College.

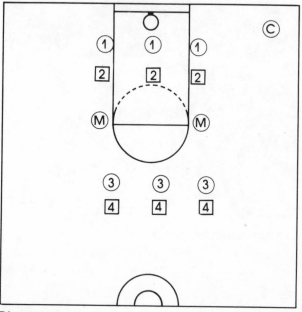

Diagram 1.

rebound or get fouled on a controlled shot, they get two points. We try to discourage team 2 from just slapping the ball out of bounds, but that can be used as a last resort to show that team 1 failed to box out properly. When 1 fails to control the rebound they move to the back of the line and team 2 becomes the defensive rebounding team, with team 3 moving to the offense.

We go through three complete rounds each day, usually requiring about ten minutes of practice time. The winning team each day gets a three-minute break while the three remaining teams run sprints.

POINTS OF EMPHASIS

1. Box your man outside the lane.
2. The offensive team cannot push the defensive team. This is a foul and the defensive team is credited with a point just as if they had cleared the rebound.
3. Encourage players to dive for loose balls.
4. The defensive team should always have position advantage. The offensive team should try to take away that advantage with constant movement.

This drill will greatly improve all facets of your team's rebounding. The competition is fierce and the improved skills are obvious.

REBOUND GAME CHART

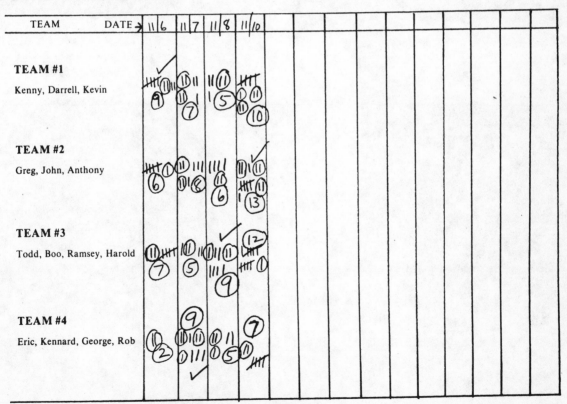

TEAM	DATE →	11/6	11/7	11/8	11/10									

TEAM #1 Kenny, Darrell, Kevin

TEAM #2 Greg, John, Anthony

TEAM #3 Todd, Boo, Ramsey, Harold

TEAM #4 Eric, Kennard, George, Rob

RULES: 1. Circle all offensive rebounds, whether scored as one point or two.
2. Stay in defensive position as long as you maintain ball control.
3. Team with most total points after three rounds is winner.

Andre Moore, Loyola University of Chicago.

6
BIG MAN BASICS

DEVELOPING AGILITY AND REACTION IN THE BIG MAN

Rich Grawer
St. Louis University

Since the multi-purpose area of the court is where the outcome of a basketball game is determined, it is of utmost importance to have a post player who can react well, is coordinated, and shows some agility. Reaction involves quick movement and shifting; coordination involves bringing different parts of the body into a working harmony; and agility requires easy motion with a minimum of strain.

The drills outlined here are designed for the pivot man but will also benefit the other members of the squad.

JUMPING DRILLS

Jumping requires coordination and agility. We place great emphasis on rope jumping. We stress jumping not because we believe it is the key to rebounding but because we feel that it helps coordination and agility.

Continuous Jumping. We do a lot of continuous jumping drills to build endurance. The player simply jumps, holding a basketball directly above his head with both hands. He goes off both feet and keeps this up for two to five minutes. We have jumped continuously for up to 10 minutes. We often play music over the loudspeakers or allow the players to talk to take their minds off the monotony.

Jumping with Bricks. To increase arm strength, we have our post man jump with a brick in each hand. This is much more difficult than simply holding a basketball. The amount of time here has to be cut drastically; even two minutes is very taxing.

Jumping Sequence. The player jumps 25 times off both feet, arms extended up in the air. We allow a slight rotation of the hands as the shoulders lower to help propel the body upward. The player next jumps 25 times off the right foot. He then jumps 25 times off the left foot. Next, 25 jumps bringing the knees up as close as possible to the chest. Then 25 jumps kicking the heels to the buttocks. And last, 25 spread-eagle jumps, touching fingers to toes in mid-air. The legs are greatly strengthened by these jumps, endurance is built up, and coordination and agility are both increased.

Diagonal Rope Jump. This drill adds a degree of difficulty to each jump. Simply tie a rope near the floor at one end and higher at the other end. The post man must jump over and back as far along the rope as possible. He does this for 20 seconds.

Second-Effort Drill. Determine the height of the post man's jump and mark that spot either on the backboard or the rim with a small piece of colored tape. The player stands under the board and jumps to touch that spot as many times as he can. He must use the touch-and-go method—no stagger steps or gather steps. You'd be surprised how this helps increase the vertical jump as well as develops great second, third, and fourth efforts.

Board-Reaction Drill. The player touches his spot on the board, but now he runs to the free throw line and touches it with his hand between every jump.

Knock-Knock Drill. The player starts from the free throw line, sprints toward the hoop, jumps, and touches his hand on the rim twice. A player who can hit the rim three times or more is a well-coordinated individual.

Hang-Time Drill. The player starts from the top of the key and sprints toward the hoop. He jumps at the bottom of the circle and tries to touch the rim. Next, he jumps

at the free throw line and tries to hit the rim.

All of our jumping drills are designed to help leg, arm, and body coordination and agility in our post man. We use one or two of these daily.

REACTION DRILLS

Too often coaches simply want to teach their post men how to shoot and what moves to make inside. We feel that we must develop good reactions in our players first. Good reaction implies quick, sure hands and legs that move quickly and under control at all times. Good hands are essential to the post man: he must catch poorly thrown passes, pick up loose balls, rebound, outlet, get a hand up in the face of a shooter, stop penetration. He must also run down court under control at all times. He must jump under control to avoid unnecessary fouls. And he must post up effectively, using his legs and body. Finally, he must be able to bend the knees, stay down, and play good post defense.

Pivoting. This is one fundamental that needs much work and is often taken for granted. A player, especially the post man, must know how to pivot. He uses the pivot to get open inside, to protect the ball when thrown inside, and to make his move to the basket.

The way we teach the pivot is quite basic. The player runs from the 10-second line to the free throw line and comes to a jump-stop—both feet parallel, knees flexed, hands out in front of him, palms facing the baseline. On the whistle, he makes a well-balanced reverse pivot off the right foot and maintains his jump-stop stance. There should be a whip-like action of the non-pivot leg as it pulls around on the pivot. The post man must be physical and not be afraid of contact.

The player alternates pivot feet and repeats the process again. As the player improves, we emphasize reaction to the whistle and more quickness in the pivot.

Once we are satisfied with the skeleton form of the pivot we add a defensive player. Now the offensive player must step into the defender, make contact, and with the hips lowered and knees bent, execute a reverse pivot by thrusting the non-pivot leg around and across the defender. The defense is told to be relatively passive in this phase of the drill.

In the third phase of the sequence there is a man at the 10-second line with a basketball. The post man 1 and the defender 2 line up as shown in Diagram 1. As the offensive player 3 moves toward the free throw line, 1 executes a reverse pivot as the defense tries to fight around him. And 3 passes the basketball to 1 as he completes his pivot. The ball should be thrown about one count prior to the pivot. It is almost like a timing pattern along the sideline in football.

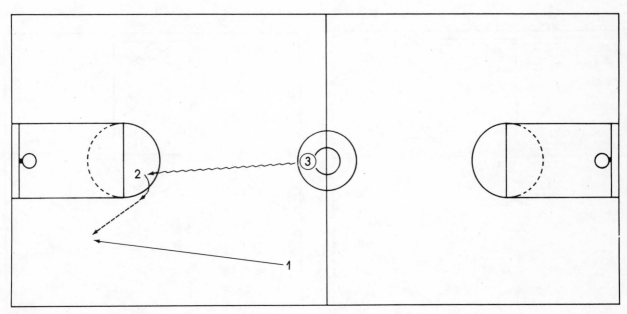

Diagram 1.

Big Man Basics

Cut-and-Go Drill. The floor is marked with tape as indicated in Diagram 2. The player hits each "X" with the outside foot, plants it firmly, and pushes off in a quick change of direction. Sounds easy? Well, it isn't. It involves concentration and coordination.

Body Obstacle Race. The squad is divided into two teams. The players lie on the floor on their backs in a straight line as indicated in Diagram 3. They should initially be five to six feet apart. The first player in each line runs and jumps over his teammates to the end of the line and returns by the same route to his original position, where he flops to the floor on his back and yells for the next player to begin. This procedure continues until all players have run the relay.

The distance between the bodies on the floor can be varied, making timing and coordination more difficult. The players could jump with feet together—a pull-up jump. The relay could be run backward. All of these variations are fun and serve to increase the foot coordination and agility of team members.

Basketball Pick-Up. The positions for

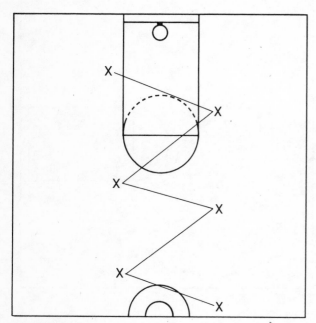

Diagram 2.

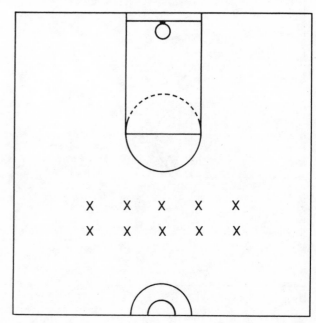

Diagram 3.

this drill are shown in Diagram 4. Player 2 is positioned six to eight feet in front of Player 1, who rolls the ball to the left of 2 so that 2 has to slide about eight to ten feet to pick it up. Player 2 returns the ball to Player 1 and begins to slide laterally in the opposite direction. Player 1 then rolls the ball about eight to ten feet to his right. This continues for 20 seconds. After the players are acquainted with the drill, a second basketball is added. Not only must the man sliding and picking up the ball concentrate and work harder, but now the man rolling the ball must be quick, for as he rolls one ball in one direction, another ball is returning from the other direction.

Blind Catch. The post player 5 stands at the middle post with his back to the coach. The coach passes the ball toward the post man and simultaneously shouts a warning. The player executes a quick jump-turn, locates the ball, catches it cleanly, and powers to the basket. The coach can also roll the ball, bounce it at the player's feet, or hurl it straight up in the air. Another variation is to pass the ball first and then shout. If he doesn't turn quickly and get those arms and hands ready to catch the ball, it will get him first.

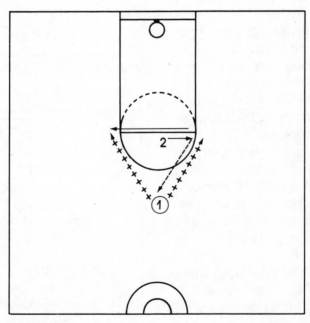

Diagram 4.

React and Block. As shown in Diagram 5, player 5 is the post man, and 1 is holding a basketball. Other squad members line up out of bounds, each holding a ball. Player 1 rolls his basketball toward the opposite free throw line at the juncture where it meets the circle *(Diagram 6)*. He immediately chases after it. As soon as the ball hits the floor, the post man slides across the lane to the first free throw mark *(Diagram 7)*, touches it with his hand or foot, and moves up the lane to touch the second free throw mark. In the meantime, 1 has picked up the basketball at the free throw line and drives in for a layup. The post man, after touching his marks, now must either block the shot, get in front of 1 and draw the charge, or harass him so that he misses the shot.

We vary the drill by allowing 1 to shoot the jumper from the free throw line, forcing our post man to react to a different situation. A third variation is to allow the second man in line 2 to join the drill and create a two-on-one situation *(Diagram 8)*.

Shot Blocker. The post man 5 is in a defensive position facing offensive players 1, 2, and 3 with his back to 4, who is out of bounds with the ball *(Diagram 9)*. Player 5 must react to a pass in bounds to any one of the three offensive players, who are instructed, upon receiving the pass, to power toward the basket.

One-on-One Mirror. The post man lines up eyeball to eyeball with another player. The other player moves laterally back and forth and the post man moves with him, always keeping as close to his teammate as possible.

Low Post Defensive Reaction. The defensive post man must guard 4 and 6, who remain stationary on the blocks *(Diagram 10)*. Players 1, 2, and 3, who also remain stationary, pass the ball around the perimeter and try to feed it inside to either

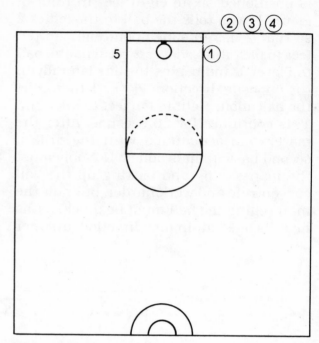

Diagram 5.

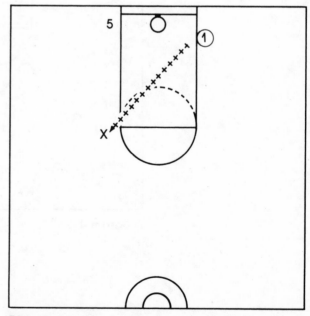

Diagram 6.

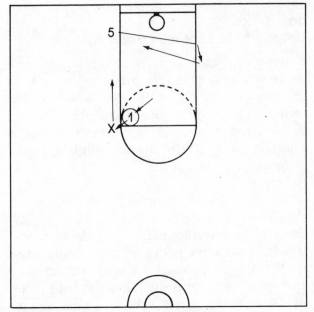

Diagram 7.

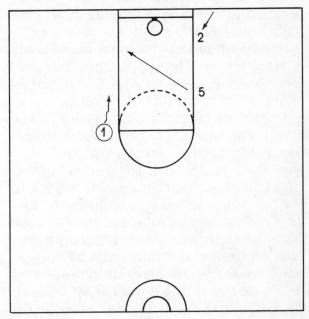

Diagram 8.

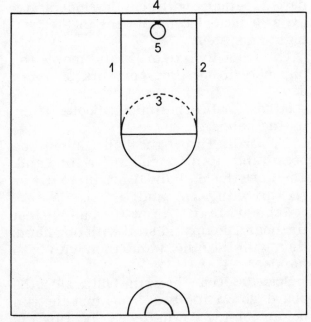

Diagram 9.

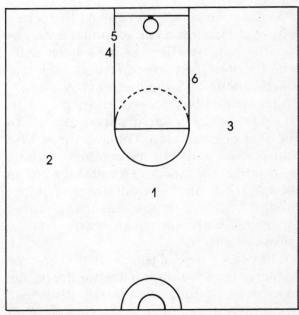

Diagram 10.

Big Man Basics

low post man for a shot. Player 5 should be on the baseline side when the ball is in the possession of 2 or 3 and on the high side, between his man and the ball, when the ball is out front in possession of 1.

Combo Shooting. The post man shoots a right-handed layup, catches the ball from the net and shoots a left-handed layup. After retrieving the ball from the net again, he takes a big stride back on the right side and shoots a short right-handed hook. He catches the ball as it goes through the net, steps back toward the right side of the goal with his back to the baseline, and pushes off his right foot as he shoots a left-handed buttonhook from the right side. Then he shoots a left-handed hook and a right-handed buttonhook from the left side. He repeats this drill twice, shooting a total of 12 shots. If the ball hits the floor, if a shot is missed, if his timing and footwork are off, or if he takes steps, he must repeat the entire sequence.

As part of our reaction and agility series with the post man, we emphasize catching the ball. We use the toss back drill, which forces the player to react quickly to a fast rebound off the toss back. We deliberately throw bad passes to the player in the post position—at his feet, way off to the side, or extra high. Then we throw him bad passes while he is moving—a flash post across the lane and a wide lane cut as if he were filling the outside lane on a fast break. Next, we repeat the same three exercises with the post man wearing gloves or mittens.

These are some of the drills that we use to increase coordination and agility in our players. Although we classify these as jumping and reaction drills, they develop our post man into the multi-purpose type of player we want him to be.

BIG MAN DRILLS AND MOVES

Joe B. Hall
University of Kentucky (retired)

During my years at Kentucky, our system was extremely effective with the use of two big men in the same lineup. We began by using Bob Guyette (6'9") and Rick Robey (6'11") together and then were fortunate enough to win the national championship with Mike Phillips (6'10") and Rick Robey.

Despite the ever-present criticism of this type of system, we worked extremely hard with our big men on a daily basis through various fundamental drills and inside moves. Toward the end of each season you can actually see the big-man drills working effectively in game situations. The secret is (1) repetition and hard work in the drill sessions each and every day; (2) patience with slow developers; and (3) a dedicated commitment to the two-big-man system.

The following are drills and moves the big men in our program work on every day.

Mikan Drill. Continuous hooks, alternating hands.

Tip Drill. Throw the ball against the board and tip it in with the right hand. Then use the left hand. Work up to five or six tips with each hand.

Rebound Stuff. Throw the ball against the board, go up and stuff with one hand, then with the other hand, then with both hands.

Beat-the-Rim. Throw the ball against the board, go up and beat it against the rim before coming down. Repeat, beating the rim twice, then three times.

Power Up. Throw the ball against the

board and bring it down to shoulder level only. Then go up very strong and shoot a power layup off the glass.

Pump Fake-Power Layup. Same as power layup, only this time use a pump fake with the head and ball. Do both these drills on each side of the basket.

Superman Rebound. Stand outside the free throw lane and throw the ball against the board above the basket at an angle. Rebound it on the other side of the lane with both feet outside of the lane. Pull ball into chin, then throw it back to the other side and rebound it. Do this continuously for 30 seconds; work up to a minute.

Two-Ball Superman. Place a ball on each block. Pick up a ball from one side and power it to the basket; quickly get the other ball and power it to the basket. Continue this sequence for 30 seconds; work up to a minute. You will need two other people to help with this drill.

BIG MAN MOVES

Low-Side Power Move. Post up on the block. The defense is ¾ fronting you on the high side. Ward him off with your left arm, take the pass, and power straight to the basket without a dribble. Then dribble once in your power move. Go up strong! Do this on both sides.

High-Side Lane Hook. Defense is now ¾ fronting on the low side. Ward him off with the right arm, spread wide, give a big target, take the pass, and take one step in the lane for the baby hook. Do this on both sides.

Lob Pass Play. Defense is totally fronting. Get position on the block. When the lob pass is thrown, keep both hands high; then when the ball is directly overhead, move away from the defensive man and get the ball for a power layup. Keep hands high to avoid a pushing-off call.

Turn and Face. Defense is playing completely behind. Establish position with a post-up. Receive the pass, pivot, and face your man. If he is pressuring you, drive him right or left, or shoot a jumper. If not, shoot a quick turn-around bank shot.

Bernard Jackson (right), Loyola University of Chicago.

7
DEFENSIVE FUNDAMENTALS

THE MULTIPLE DEFENSE

Most modern teams apply a multiple defense, which means they use a combination of man-to-man, zones, presses, match-ups, whatever it takes to confuse and befuddle an opponent while providing flexibility.

Basically, today's coach selects a half-court defense as his operating base. He teaches a press for use in dire situations or for a change of pace. Then he adds a second half-court defense to have options and more flexibility.

All players should be drilled in basic man-to-man defenses so that they are capable of beating their individual opponents. They should also be trained to recognize two- and three-man moves. The success of every defense is built on individual players properly executing the fundamentals.

The basic stance is a boxer's stance, wide enough to prevent a player from driving around him. Weight should be kept on the front foot to allow the defender to push off to protect against the drive.

The great defensive player must have a certain attitude. He must be determined and hard-nosed. He must feel that any time an offensive player beats him, it's an affront to his humanity, his pride.

MAN-TO-MAN DEFENSE

Clarence Burch
Lycoming College

There is no easy way to play man-to-man defense. It certainly isn't the fun part of basketball. We play defense in order to get the ball as quickly as possible so we can play offense. We know our defense beyond eight passes: the movement involved with this many passes could force an individual breakdown someplace in our defensive structure. So we play defense with great intensity before such a breakdown can occur. The 45-second clock might be a bonus for the active defensive team.

Our team defense actually starts with a one-on-one, man-to-man defense. The most difficult task for a defensive player to handle is a one-on-one situation at the top of the key when the offensive player still has all his weapons—the pass, dribble, and shot. In this situation we teach our defense to take half the offense away by overplaying the ball handler's strong side and shooting hand. This now becomes a different challenge for the offensive player: he can no longer make a move causing the defensive man to react by transferring his weight. The defense, by proper positioning, has made a difficult defensive task realistic and can now contain the offense.

The defense now controls the offensive direction and has greatly reduced the offense's options. He must eventually go to his weak side. Even if he gets a half-step on the defense, he is still going to his weak side; when he stops, the defense is on his shooting-hand side, which usually prevents the shot. The defense can move with greater confidence and more speed because it controls the direction.

DEFENSIVE ALIGNMENT (SEE DIAGRAM)

Player X1 forces the offense to the side. Player X2 is in a split taking the passing lane away from 2. Player X3 is one pass away in a prevent position. Player X5 is one pass away in the high post area. In this first phase the defense allows the offense the back door from a variety of positions. The back door is not a gift. The

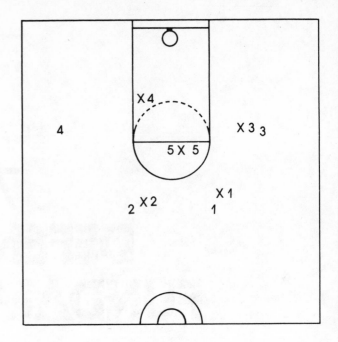

offense still has to work for this move; but the move is there, and the defense knows it. We have given offense this direction, and we can take it away.

If 2 should go back door, X4 is in a position to stop his direction and the pass, if 1 has the courage to throw such a pass. If 3 makes the back door move on X3, X4 moves over to stop 3 and X3 joins X4 in the area of the baseline, which further reduces the offense's options. If 5 goes back door, X4 again is in support position and will cut him off.

Meanwhile, pressure from X1 makes it difficult for 1 to make the back-door pass or dribble to his strong side. And 3, 2, or 5 must move further away from the basket in order to get the initial pass.

MATCH-UP DEFENSE

Clarence Gaines
Winston-Salem State University

I try to teach the match-up to my staff and our youngsters in my own way. I just call it "understanding." One of my most talented teams ended up with a mediocre record because there wasn't enough communication and understanding among all persons concerned.

Coaches and players must understand each other. With the broad coverage given basketball teams by the media, a lot of jealousies exist. If an athlete's performance merits television, radio, and newspaper coverage, or any other plaudits, then he deserves it. It is the coach's responsibility to see that this does not interfere with his program by causing ill feelings among the kids or ill feelings with the faculty. We have a monumental task to perform in the development of a complete person, and opportunities only come to those who are prepared.

We have used the match-up zone very successfully for the last eight or ten years.

The first thing that I try to get across to every youngster is that at one time or another in our defense, everybody's going to be the point man. We line up every time in a 1–2–2 *(Diagram 1)*. Now if anybody's dumb enough to come down without movement or to put a man in the bucket, we stay in this zone. We don't do a lot of arm-waving and that sort of thing.

When the ball is out front, we want 1 to have a man-to-man attitude, almost a pressure attitude, because we don't want him to allow the ball handler to have an easy pass. So I come out with a triangle *(Diagram 2)*. When the ball is rotated, I'm going to end up with a triangle and a square.

We're not like most coaches who hold up cards or call out numbers. We don't have any plays. We have four offensive sets, and we try to do what we can according to what the defense does. There's no need fighting a defense at all.

When the ball is rotated toward 2 our players move *(Diagram 3)*. Let the kids play with it; you'll be surprised how they discover for themselves new areas where they should be or how to close off the passing lanes.

The only drills we use with these guys involve the conditioning process. They've got to learn to play a man full court. So we actually teach the full-court defense and full-court offense to improve conditioning and develop an attitude before we go into any patterns. They dribble one-on-one full court first.

We have a few basic rules in the match-up. If we get caught in a transition situation, 1 tries to contain and hold off. In this

Defensive Fundamentals

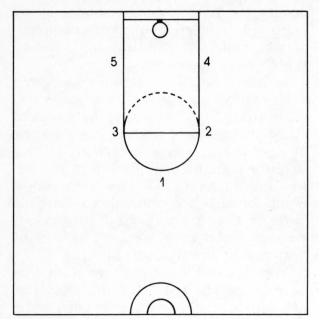

Diagram 1.

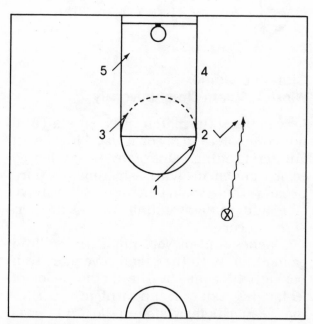

Diagram 2.

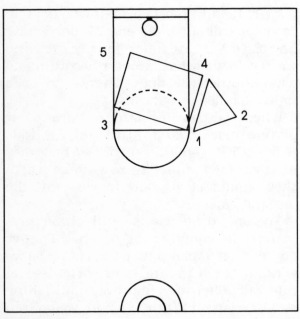

Diagram 3.

Diagram 4.

alignment we run across a lot of stack offenses, with no one in the post and a man on the side. Then we use a 1-3-1 zone. We don't have a kid cover both baselines like they do in some zones.

Ninety percent of the time the ball gets inside on offense, it goes to the floor. We drill against this in practice. Every time the ball goes on the floor, we clobber the guy in the middle who puts it on the floor and there is no foul called. After a while, the message gets across that the coach wants rapid ball movement.

Our league uses a 30-second shot clock, so we don't have to play defense for three or four minutes. I try to get across to these youngsters that the other team has to shoot the ball in 30 seconds. If everybody busts a gut, it will be pretty easy to get the 30 seconds over with.

Another rule is that if the ball is dribbled to the corner, the moment the man puts the ball on the floor three times, our defender goes into a man-to-man defense and guards him *(Diagram 4)* until a shot is taken.

We never widen out our triangle and square too much, because we don't want the offense to find an easy way to get the ball into the middle.

THE LOUISVILLE PRESS

Denny Crum
University of Louisville

The key to Louisville's success is our defense and the ability to control the tempo of the game, two factors that go hand in hand on the court. By using a full-court press and a switching man-to-man defense, we can speed up the game and put pressure on the opponent.

THE 2-2-1 PRESS

The objective of the press is to speed up the tempo. You can change the 2–2–1 press to run it different ways, based on what the offense does to attack. An ideal pressing team includes a player (1) with quick hands, good height, and lateral movement to contain the dribbler. Player 2 has to be capable of following directions and be able to contain the offense. Being able to trap the offense with the assistance of 1 is vital for the tallest and quickest forward, player 3. It is best for player 4 to be left-handed so that he can position himself to be involved in more interceptions with his strong hands and quick anticipation. And the "general," player 5, must have good judgment and be an excellent communicator, for he has the best view of the floor and directs the press.

The responsibilities of 1 are to always have his hands up, playing a half-step in front of the ball to the inside while favoring the middle. This causes the ball to go to the sideline. Player 2 retreats to the middle of the floor when the ball is on the side so that he can intercept any passes back to the middle. While trapping opponents on the sides with 1, 3 is the bluffing and retreating man, never letting the ball go over his head. Anticipating the pass and looking to intercept is the responsibility of 4, while 5 adjusts to the ball side, letting nothing go by him, and acting as the last line of defense if the press is broken.

THE BEST AREAS TO PRESS

The best areas to press are just across the 10-second line (Area 1), just before the 10-second line (Area 2), and in the corners on the offensive end (Area 3) *(Diagram 1)*.

Most trapping occurs in Area 1 *(Diagram 2)*. Player 2 is in the gap area to stop the "tweeners," passes between the trapped player and the offensive player in front of the trap. When the dribbler stops, the press traps in Area 2. Remember to play the pass when trapping, because the closer the defense is to the offense, the easier it is for the offense to pass around the defense. Play one to one and a half steps off the man with the ball to force him to pass over you.

If the ball happens to get by you, get

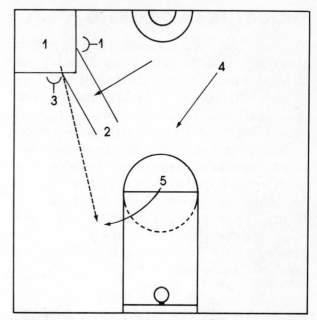

Diagram 2.

back in front of it. Don't foul, because it stops the clock and slows down the tempo. Try not to let the ball go in the middle—this is the best place for the offense to attack the press.

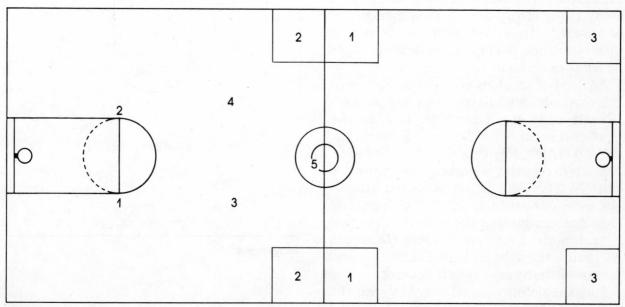

Diagram 1.

THOUGHTS ON PRESSING

No press can steal the ball every time. But there are many reasons to use this type of defense. Players love to press and fans love to watch it. A press at the beginning of the game can cause a turnover which relaxes your players and puts extra pressure on your opponents. It is a great conditioner, allows a coach to use more players, and teaches anticipation which is carried over to other defensive plays. Most importantly, the press sets the tempo and edges your opponents out of their offensive strategies, forcing them to do things they don't normally do.

VARIATIONS OF THE 2-2-1 PRESS

The **straight 2-2-1 press** (Diagram 3) forces the dribble to the sideline. Trapping and cheating toward the middle forces the offense pass back across the floor in front of you and slows down the game.

Players 1 and 2 deny the in-bounds pass while 3 and 4 prevent anyone in their areas from receiving the ball in the **2-D** or **Deny** press (Diagram 4). This causes the offense to throw over your heads, which gives you time to come from behind to get in front of the ball.

Against a tandem (Diagram 5), guard the man who goes to your side of the floor. If both go to the same side, 1 takes the first cutter on his side while 2 takes the second cutter; vice-versa on the other side.

Switch against a screen (Diagrams 6 and 7). The man being screened guards the screener and the original defender of the screener guards the cutter.

And against a triple tandem (Diagram 8), match up with all three. Players 3 and 4 should then move up on defense.

You, the defense, must stay between the offense and the ball at all times. Any time the ball does enter the middle of the court,

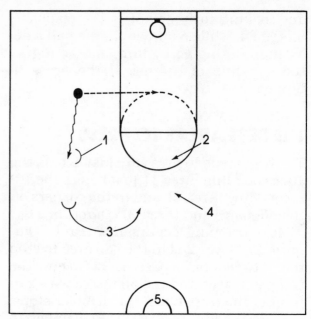
Diagram 3.

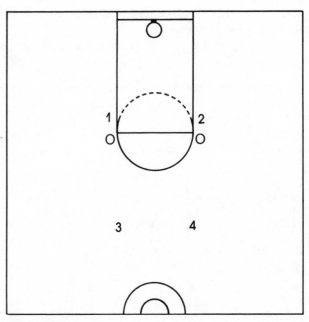
Diagram 4.

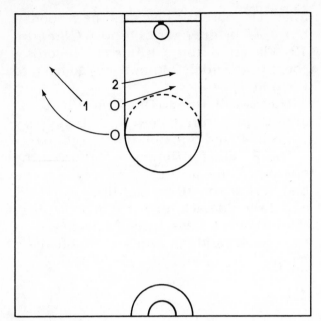

Diagram 5.

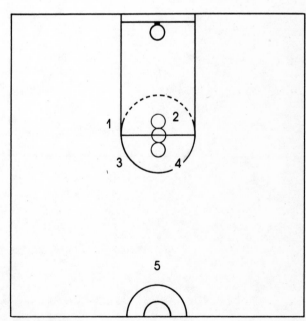

Diagram 6.

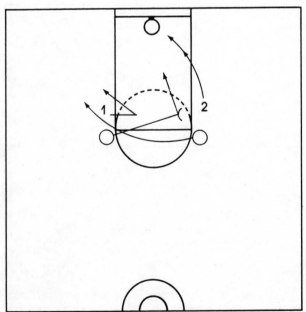

Diagram 7.

Diagram 8.

Defensive Fundamentals

get in front of it and force a pass to the sidelines or try to trap the receiver.

The **2 "Flopum"** *(Diagram 9)* involves 4 turning his back to the ball and double-teaming the offense's best ball handler. While 3 and 5 play man-to-man, 2 is as deep as their deepest man and as close to the ball as their farthest man is from the ball. Player 2 then has the responsibility for any man running long down the court *(Diagram 10)*.

The **2-1-2** press fronts the offense in the middle of the floor and prevents the pass *(Diagram 11)*. 3 fronts the middle man and forces the ball down the side-lines. The baseline becomes the responsibility of 5 before he tries to steal *(Diagram 12)*. Players 3 and 1 influence the cross-court pass which 2 knows will go back to the middle.

The **2-1-2 Deny** *(Diagram 13)* has 1 and 2 preventing the in-bounds pass while 3, 4, and 5 match up man-to-man.

The **2 "Fluff"** *(Diagram 14)* forces the offense to take about 8 seconds to get the ball across the 10-second line. Players 1 and 2 should back up a step or so to allow the in-bounds pass. This defense eats up the clock and disrupts the offense's tempo.

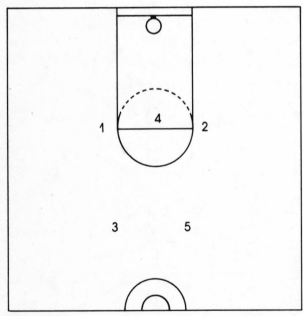

Diagram 9.

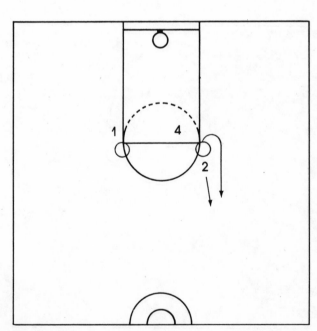

Diagram 10.

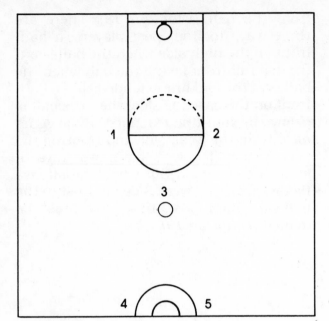

Diagram 11.

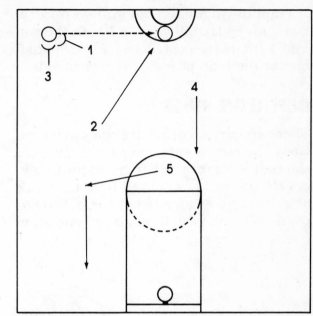

Diagram 12.

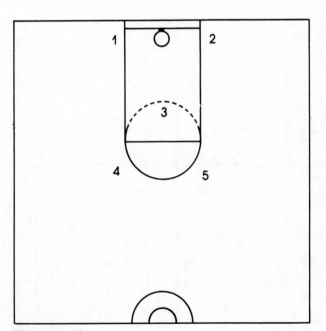

Diagram 13.

Defensive Fundamentals

Trapping in Area 3 *(Diagrams 1 and 15)* has 3 and 5 trapping while 1 is in the gap and 4 fronts the post. Player 2 is responsible for the high post and the weak side.

DEFENSIVE RULES

There are certain defensive rules to follow: Deny the strong side one pass away from the ball *(Diagram 16)*, front all post players *(Diagram 17)*, sag hard from the weak side two passes away from the ball *(Diagram 17)*, and switch on all screens away from the ball *(Diagram 18)*. There are three ways to front post players: a half-front on the high side when the ball is out front; a full front facing the ball when the ball is at the foul line extended; and a half-front on the baseline side when the ball is below the foul line extended. By sagging hard from the weak side and fronting the post, you will always have two ways of guarding the post. But when the offense flashes from the weak-side low post to the ball-side high post, this pass must be denied *(Diagram 19)*.

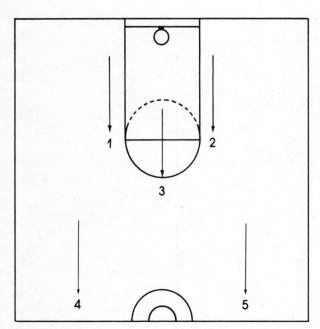

Diagram 14.

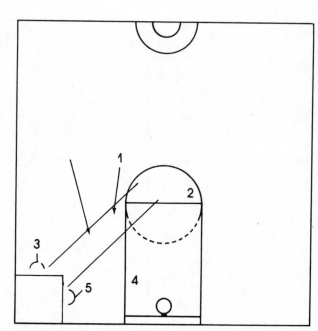

Diagram 15.

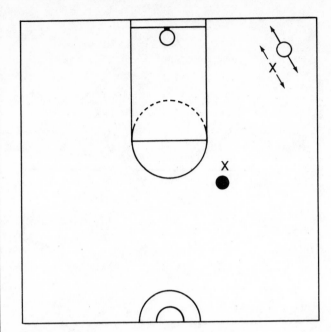

Diagram 16.

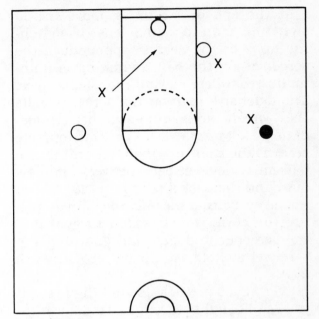

Diagram 17.

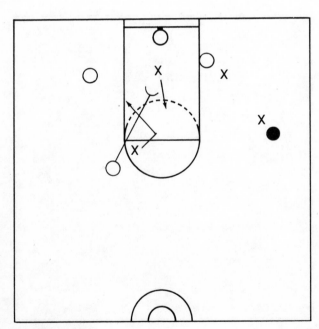

Diagram 18.

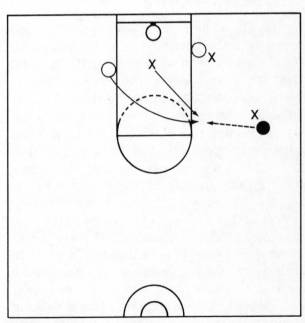

Diagram 19.

Defensive Fundamentals

At the end of the press, move into a switching man-to-man defense by matching up with the nearest opponent. If the screen is on the ball, switching is automatic, regardless of what the offense does. The defensive man on the screener calls the screen and jump-switches immediately *(Diagram 20)*. On an outside screen, the man originally guarding the ball must now get back between his new man and the basket *(Diagram 20)*. On an inside away from the ball, the man guarding the cutter must switch to guarding the screener and the man guarding the screener switches to the cutter *(Diagram 21)*.

Even if you are not a switching team, if you can't fight through, you have to switch. So why not switch in the first place?

OTHER THOUGHTS

Louisville is defense-oriented to stop opponents from getting the ball inside. We play man-to-man with zone principles so that we take away what our opponents want to do; we try to deny their ball reversal and force the back-door move. Very few teams switch on defense like Louisville. Since our opponents are not used to this type of defense, we can confuse them easily. We recommend getting a shot off during the transition because it provides better rebounding opportunities and the shot is usually unguarded. (It must be at least a 50 percent shot.) Also, it's good to hide your players' weaknesses and make sure they know their strengths very well.

Louisville doesn't spend time studying opponents because we will play the same no matter who the opponents are or how they play. Louisville concentrates on itself.

Diagram 20.

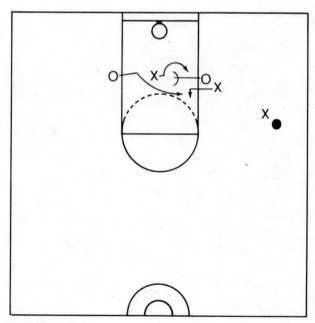

Diagram 21.

WILDCAT BASKETBALL

Joe B. Hall
University of Kentucky (retired)

The three most important factors to consider on defense are your opponents' shooting percentage, the number of second shots your opponents get, and the number of offensive turnovers you have. You must take away the favorite shot from the best shooter and eliminate any second shot possibilities from the offense.

SIX-WEEK PRESEASON CONDITIONING PROGRAM

We lift weights three days a week and run three days for strength and tone, not bulk. We run 220s under 32 seconds at forced intervals of one and a half minutes, adding one 220 each day to a total of 15. We believe this teaches the players the capabilities of the human body and the ability to break the pain barrier.

Our best weight exercise is the "clean," but we also use half squats, toe rises, leg extensions, step-ups, leg curls, splits, and bench jumps to help tone the body. Strength is important to individual defense and the player who lacks ability can sometimes overpower the offense with his strength. Therefore, we believe that the superstar can also benefit from weight training.

DEFENSIVE PHILOSOPHY

To be an effective defending team you need both full-court man-to-man and zone defenses, but the man-to-man defense is basic for a sound defensive system. We use a 1–3–1 or a 2–3 zone as a change-up. Surprisingly some very good teams don't handle zones well. You also need to teach special defenses like the box-and-1, the triangle-and-2, the run-and-jump, and three-quarter court traps. Even if you don't spend much time on these defenses, it is important to know how to attack with them.

DEFENDING THE STARS

The opponents' offensive rebounds are the most important half-time statistic. Usually the star of the opposing team greatly affects this number. Keep the ball away from the star as often as possible. Know his favorite moves and patterns and how he gets his shots. Make him do something he doesn't want to do. Since many stars are low-post threats, figure out where you can get help, who can you sag, and how you can put pressure on him so that this player will be less of a threat.

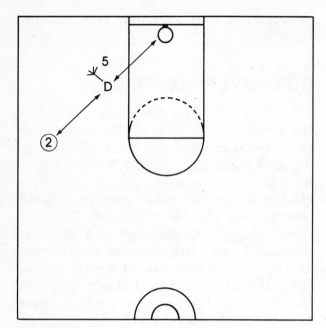

Diagram 1.

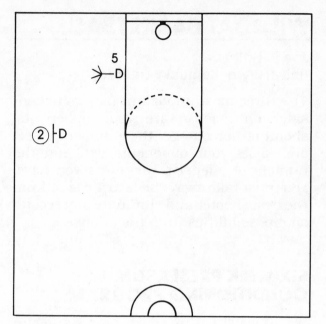

Diagram 2.

DEFENDING THE LOW POST

Don't let the low post man take a position on "the line," the imaginary line between the ball and the basket *(Diagram 1)*. Take the high side away from the passer and defend the feeder squared up to the side-line, forcing him baseline. This removes one passing lane and helps defend the low post.

Get in front of the low post man *(Diagram 2)*. We like for him to "step through" and then pivot. Put pressure on the passer while giving defensive help from the perimeter.

KENTUCKY OFFENSE

We run a **strong side offense** *(Diagram 3)*. The ball handler 1 passes and goes to the corner as an alternate feeder or shooter. The power guard 2 goes opposite of 1; they stay 12 to 15 feet apart. So that he can shoot or feed to the low post, the quick forward 3 goes to the top of the key after the first pass. Acting as a receiver or as a feeder, the power forward 4 comes off the down-screen by the center 5 who posts "on line" in the low post.

On the **weak-side reverse** *(Diagram 4)*, 4 reverses the ball to 2 and crosses to the opposite wing. Player 2 dribbles to the weak side looking for 4. Cutting to the deep post and to the corner is 3, and 5 crosses over and sets up the low post "on line" with 4. Player 1 cuts to the top of the key.

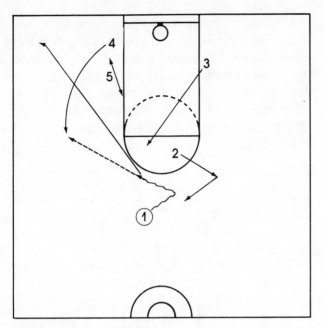

Diagram 3.

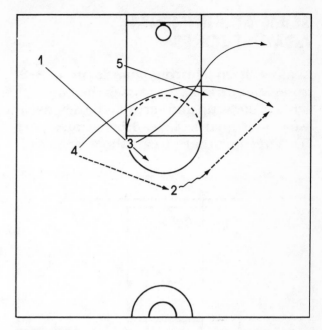

Diagram 4.

When getting a weak-side sag *(Diagram 5)*, 3 sets an inside screen for 4 who dribbles over 3 to pick up 2's sagging defensive man. Then 4 can feed 2 going to the basket. If nothing develops, 5 rolls to

the weak side and 4 reverses the ball to 2 and shuffle-cuts to the low post off the inside screen from 3 *(Diagram 6)*. Player 2 brings the ball around to 5, who then feeds 4 on the shuffle cut.

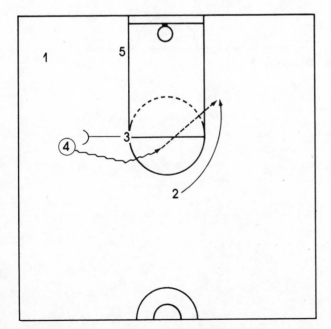

Diagram 5.

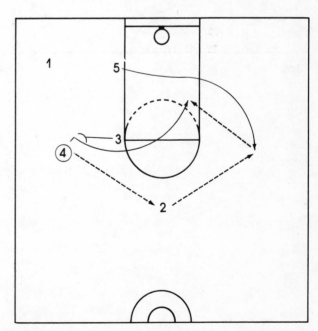

Diagram 6.

Defensive Fundamentals

SOME ADJUSTMENTS AGAINST ZONES

Against **hard shifting guards in a 2-3 zone** (*Diagram 7*), 2 reverses the ball to 1 while 5 steps up and screens the defensive weak-side guard. Player 1 penetrates past 5's screen so that he can shoot, feed 3 on the wing, or feed 4 on the low post.

If the opposing team uses a **pressing 2-3 zone** (*Diagram 8*), 5 gets the ball and sets up "on line" with 3. Coming to the ball is 4 as 2 goes to the hole on the foul line created by the defensive weak-side guard playing the passing line from 3 back to 1.

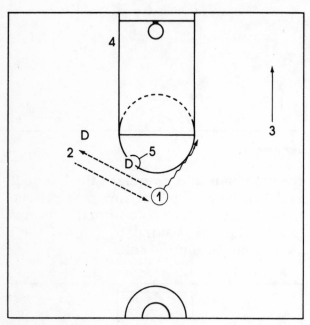

Diagram 7.

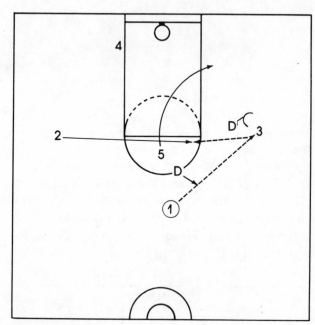

Diagram 8.

Against a **tight 2-3 zone** *(Diagram 9)*, 3 returns the ball to 1 while 2 screens the weak-side defensive guard. As 1 receives the ball over the screen by 2, he looks for 4 or 5 playing low.

A **2-1-2 against a match-up zone** *(Diagram 10)* can be effective by having 1 go through to the opposite corner after passing to 3, who then reverses the ball to 2 and flashes to the high post when 4 receives the pass from 2. Rolling to the opposite side of the first pass, 5 screens for 1 cutting along the baseline. Player 5 then rolls to the low post "on line" with the ball. Either 5, 1, or 3 can now receive the pass from 4.

On the **reversal** against a match-up *(Diagram 11)*, 4 reverses to 2, gets the return pass on the opposite wing, and feeds to 5 or 3. We like to get the ball to 5 on the dotted circle.

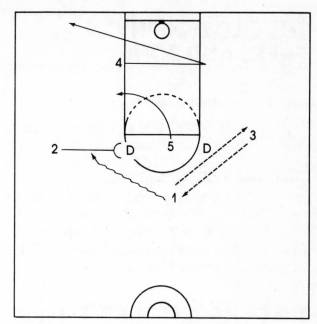

Diagram 9.

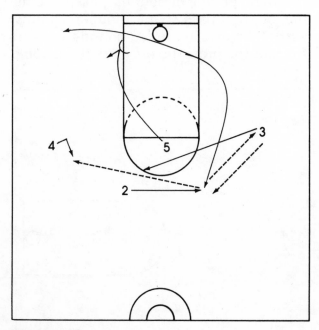

Diagram 10.

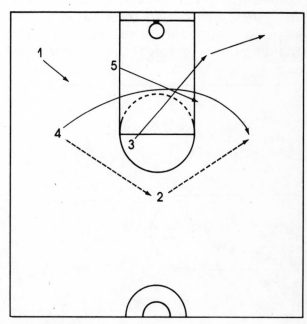

Diagram 11.

Defensive Fundamentals

THE OLD DOMINION PRESS AND ZONE

Paul Webb
Old Dominion University

During the past 29 years of my coaching career (19 years at Randolph-Macon College and 10 years at Old Dominion University), the 1–2–1–1 full-court press has proven to be very effective. During this time, we have obviously made some changes and adjustments depending upon the quickness, size, and talent of our players and our opponents.

THE OBJECTIVES OF A 1-2-1-1 FULL-COURT PRESS

The objectives of the 1–2–1–1 press include pressuring the ball out of bounds, double-teaming, and cutting off the passing lanes adjacent to the ball. Also, you hope to stop the penetration of the dribbler and to force the opponent to make the error; i.e., bad pass, traveling, 10-second violation, hurried shot. Unless the game situation warrants it, you do not want to foul. Do not let your opponents lay up or rebound any missed shots. Lastly, try to speed up the tempo of the game.

PLAYER POSITIONS AND RESPONSIBILITIES

Each player has specific roles to play in the press *(Diagram 1)*. The strong forward 4 plays tight on the baseline. The second guard 2 and the quick forward 3 position themselves one step outside the foul line. Playing halfway between the top of the free throw circle and the mid-court circle is the point guard 1 while the center 5 is at the same position on the opposite end of the court.

The strong forward 4 tries to prevent the high or lob in-bounds pass, forcing the bounce pass. While double-teaming with 1, 2, or 3 on an in-bounds pass in front of the press, he prevents the dribble

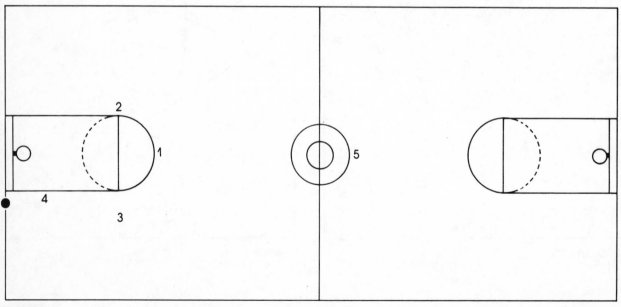

Diagram 1.

back towards the middle and does not allow the dribbler to split the double-team. Player 4 also double-teams the ball if it is thrown past him but gets in the passing lane if the ball is thrown out of the double-team not past him. He retreats to the basket as quickly as possible if he is unable to double-team.

If 2 and 3 are on the ball side of the court, they double-team the in-bounds pass, preventing the dribble up the sidelines and not allowing the dribbler to split the double-team. They double-team the ball if it is thrown out of the double-team past them and get into the passing lane if the ball is thrown out of the double-team not past them. If they are unable to double-team, they retreat to the basket as quickly as possible.

If Players 2 and 3 are on the opposite side of the ball, they cut off the pass either back towards the middle or back under the basket, whichever way is dictated by the coach. They double-team the ball if passed back to a man in their area. If no

double-team is possible, they retreat to the basket.

The point guard 1 prevents the in-bounds pass between 2 and 3 and mid-court. He cuts off the pass up court over the double-team or cuts off the pass back into the middle if his teammates are cutting off the pass back under the basket. He double-teams the ball if the pass is made up court out of the 2 and 3 double-team; if the double-team is not possible, he stops the penetration of the dribbler.

The center 5 must protect the basket. He should come out as far as he possibly can to help the defense, but his main responsibility is to prevent layups.

FORMATIONS

At Old Dominion we teach three variations of the press. In the regular press, we allow the in-bounds pass; in the over-play, we deny the in-bounds pass; and in the double-team, our point guard double-teams the opponent's best ball handler. During

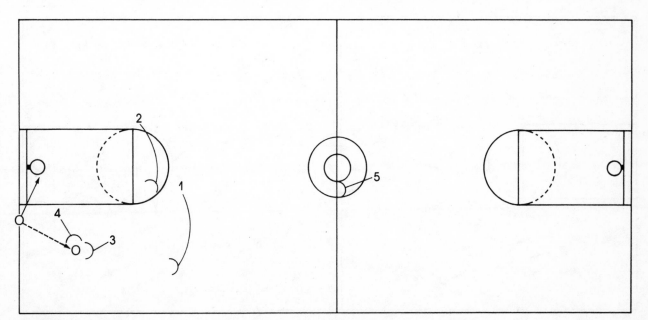

Diagram 2.

Defensive Fundamentals

the **in-bounds pass** *(Diagram 2)*, 4 forces a bounce pass and double-teams with 3. Player 2 cuts off the pass into the middle as 1 cuts off the pass over the double-team. While protecting the basket, 5 plays up in the defense as far as he can. If the ball is **passed into the lane** *(Diagram 3)*, 2 and 4 double-team and 3 cuts off the pass to the top of the key. When the ball is **passed up court** *(Diagram 4)*, 1 and 3 double-team and 2 and 4 retreat to the basket in the passing lanes.

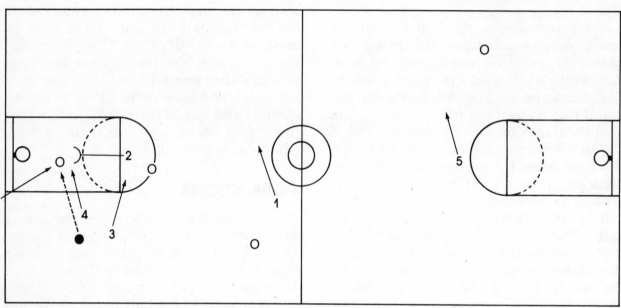

Diagram 3.

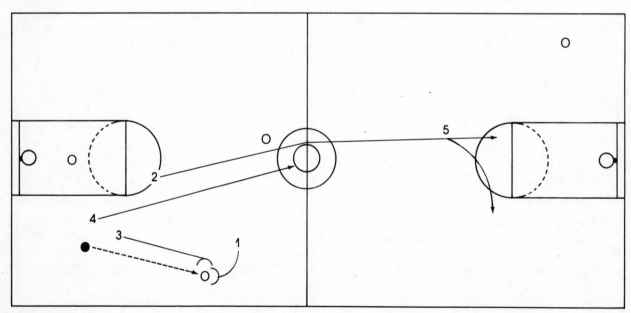

Diagram 4.

Defensive Fundamentals   102

1-2-2 ZONE DEFENSE

Diagram 5—Basic Alignment.

Diagram 6—Ball on the Wing.

Diagram 7—Ball in the Corner.

Diagram 8—Baseline Drive.

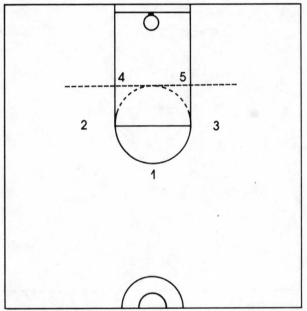

Diagram 5.

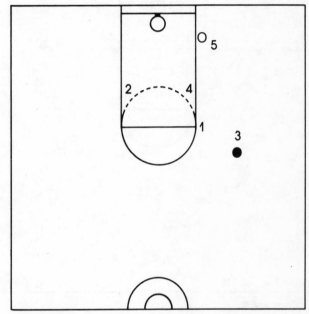

Diagram 6.

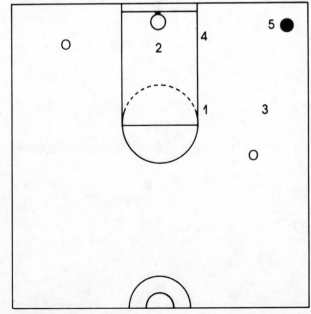

Diagram 7.

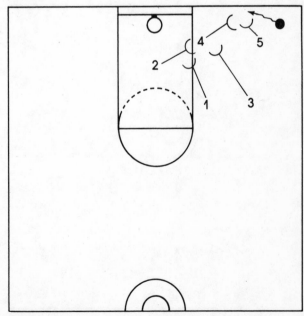

Diagram 8.

Defensive Fundamentals

Diagram 9—Cross-Court Pass.

Diagram 9A—Cross-Court Defensive Movement.

Diagram 10—Pass Directly into the High Post.

Diagram 11—Point Man Drives the Middle.

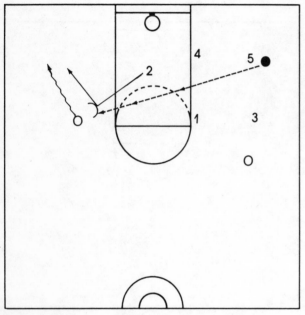

Diagram 9.

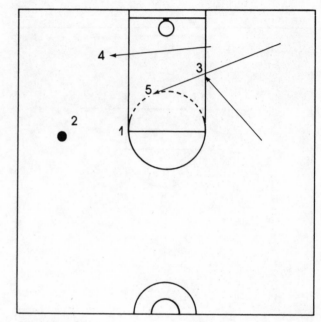

Diagram 9A.

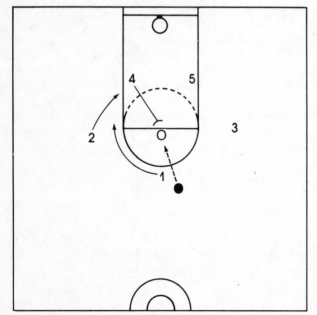

Diagram 10.

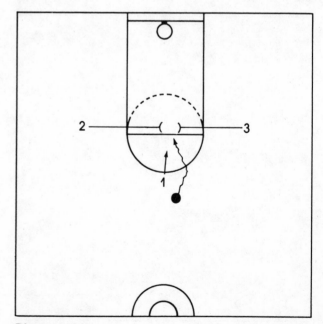

Diagram 11.

DEFENSING THE FOUR CORNERS

Norm Sloan
University of Florida

If you are going to defend against the four corners, it is a good idea to teach it as if you intend to use it in your own offensive scheme. It is foolish to wait until three days before you play a team to prepare for something a little unusual. Besides, the four corners is an excellent ball-handling drill.

The four corners offense is quite simple. One player is in each corner and the best ball handler is in the middle. It is his job to get around his defender and drive to the basket. One of the other defenders must leave his man to prevent the layup, thus creating a two-on-one situation and a probable slam dunk from the baseline.

We play our normal defense against a four corners offense unless it is near the end of the game and we are in a gambling situation. This is when we must decide when, how, and whom to double-team and whom to foul. We use the clock in practice and set up all the situations we may face in the last few minutes of a game and go over them again, again, and again.

We try to keep the ball from the player in the middle. When he dishes off the ball, we move to the ball side and deny the return

Defensive Fundamentals

pass *(Diagram 1)*. Then we force the ball down the sideline, never allowing the drive into the middle *(Diagram 2)*. We don't worry much about the over-the-top pass, a low-percentage pass that can be defended easily by moving another defen-

sive player into the front court.

When you force the ball down the side, the other defenders must rotate to the ball. The only problem is that this leaves a man in the opposite corner open for a lob pass *(Diagram 3)*. This puts a lot of pres-

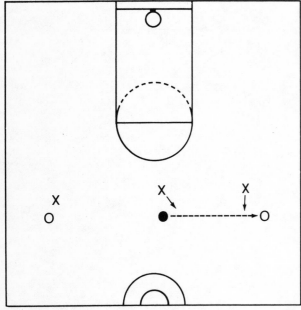

Diagram 1.

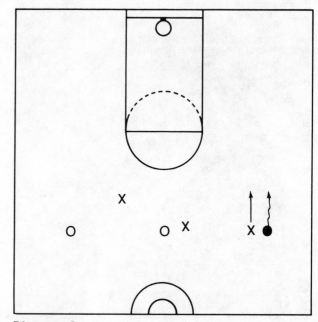

Diagram 2.

sure on the defense. It's not easy to stop the four corners!

We practice a lot of defensive situations—two-on-one, three-on-two, and so on—where our players are constantly outnumbered. This forces them to communicate and help each other *(Diagram 4)*. The offensive fouls can be the worst offensive play and the best defensive play of the game. It is one of the best ways to discourage or slow down the four corners offense *(Diagram 5)*.

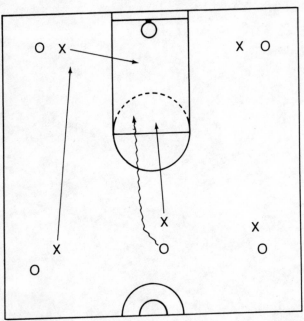

Diagram 3.

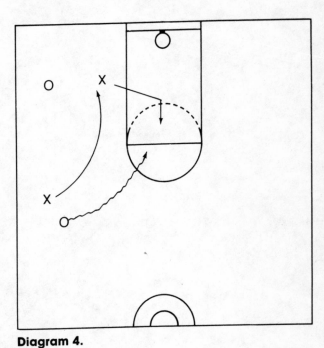

Diagram 4.

Diagram 5.

Defensive Fundamentals

Purvis Ellison (with ball), University of Louisville.

8
OFFENSIVE BASICS

WEAK-SIDE FORWARD OFFSET OFFENSE

Norm Stewart
University of Missouri

This is a game of percentages. You've got to know what works 70, 80, 90 percent of the time. You've got to have a knowledge of yourself, the players, the game, and the situation, so when that one time comes up, you can make a decision. It may not be tried and true, but you make that reaction, and if you know yourself and your players, it'll work.

If you catch yourself reaching for that 5 or 10 percent, you're not going to get it. There are no tricky plays.

The most important job you have as the coach is to select your personnel, people who are going to carry out your ideas about what you're going to do with your ball club. To me, it's like being an artist. If I'm going to paint a picture, I don't want to hand the brush to somebody else. I want it to be my picture.

There are three areas on the court. The basket area, or the block, is the first; this is where we operate. This area is where the game is dominated. The boards, rebounds, close-in scoring, point-blank range—that is the game. What player plays there? A player who has to have some size, although sometimes your basket man can be somebody who just has the ability to play around the basket, to step around somebody, to get his hands on the ball. Put that player in the basket area. What we try to do is figure out very quickly if that man can shoot. If he can't, we're going to keep him away from the ball.

The next area is what we call the mid-court. The middle-of-the-court player, I think, is the one the game was designed for: the player who can catch the ball, pass

109

the ball, put it on the floor, has fair shooting range, can make good decisions, play in a crowd; in short, probably the best player on your team. Sometimes you've got to bring him out of that area to help you bring the ball down the floor but primarily he's in the middle-of-the-court area.

The rest of the court is the perimeter area. You can talk about point guards, but I have trouble with the terms today. We just try to get players, put them together, and have one of them bring it up and throw it to the one who can shoot the best. These are the three areas we are concerned about: who is in the basket area, who is in the middle of the floor, and who are our perimeter people?

There are three stages of offense: the conversion for fast break, which leads to the easy bucket; the set, a basic form of organization; and the "in-between," a three-second period occurring perhaps 16 times a game where the chance to score occurs during the period between a missed basket on the fast break and the time it takes for the teams to set up their offenses and defenses.

We like to break. We want the easy bucket, the first stage. We feel that's the one thing we can always do. I don't care how small our ball club is, or what the situation happens to be; we can get an easy basket. We've had some slow teams—

not tremendously slow, but fairly slow in comparison to the competition. Offside running can get you a lot of buckets. To me, that is a key for conversion. How many people can you get to run without the basketball? How quickly you get the ball out doesn't have anything to do with it. That's one of the toughest assignments we have: everybody wants to break, but they all want to do it with the ball. Get that offside guy to run—that's the key. And you can run regardless of your quickness if you have mobility and ball handling.

On offense, we play a weak-side forward offset. Regardless of how we come in, we go into this offset—it's an overload. Our basic alignment is shown in Diagram 1.

Our first option at the end of the fast break is illustrated in Diagram 2: 1 passes to 2, who passes in to 5 and screens for 3; 4 and 1 clear out. Or if the middle is open, 4 can come to the ball and look for the pass from 2, as in Diagram 3.

You look for certain ways to get your best player the basketball. Ricky Frazier was a guy like that. The players knew when we had to have a shot at the end of a game, the ball was going to him. This special option (Diagram 4) was run for Frazier: Player 4 breaks high to open the basket area and Player 2 lobs to Frazier (1) for the stuff.

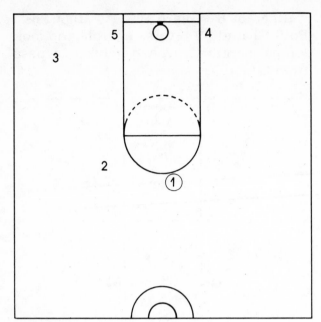

Diagram 1.

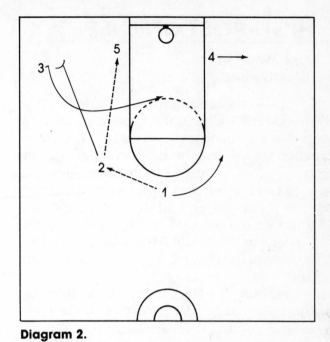

Diagram 2.

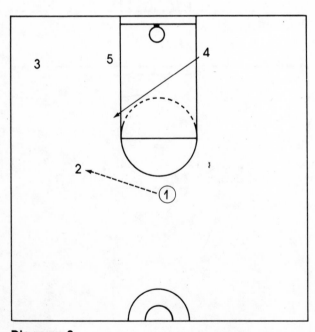

Diagram 3.

Diagram 4.

Offensive Basics

HIGH-POST OFFENSE

John Wooden
UCLA (retired)

I want shots coming from the offense, not from some individual dribbling around to get open, except in certain situations when the defense makes a mistake. I want triangle rebounding power underneath, a long rebounder, and a protector. We never pass to a player standing still and we must attack each side of the floor equally.

Diagram 1—Basic Alignment. The center starts the play on either side of the foul line.

Diagram 2—Overplay When Setting Up. F1 must be alert and cut to the post whenever the defense overplays G1 to deny the pass from G2. As G2 passes to F1, G1 cuts for the basket and F1 can pass to G1, G2 as a second cutter, or G1 coming around a double screen by C and F2.

Diagram 3—Overplay on the Strong-Side Forward. Player F2 fakes up to meet the ball against the overplay and suddenly accelerates for the basket, turning inside for the pass. If not open, he buttonhooks at the foul lane. If still not open, he crosses foul lane and comes around a double screen by C and F1 and looks for a pass from G1, who has taken a pass from G2. Never call the plays—let the defense call your plays by how they play against you.

Diagram 4—Overplay on the Strong-Side Guard. F2 screens and rolls with the same three options as Diagram 3.

Diagram 5—Two-Man Play on Reverse. G1 passes to F2 coming around the double screen and cuts for the basket, screening for G2 or getting an up-screen from G2. Player G1 may pass to G2 coming up to the side post and cut off of him for a two-man play with F2 coming on back as the protector.

Diagram 6—Guard Pass to High Post. Both F1 and F2 reverse sharply and look for pass from C, who has taken a pass from G1.

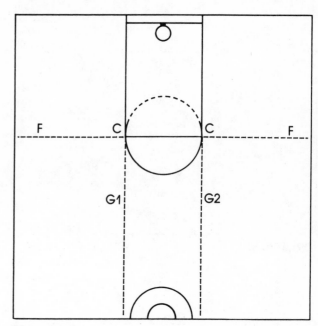

Diagram 1.

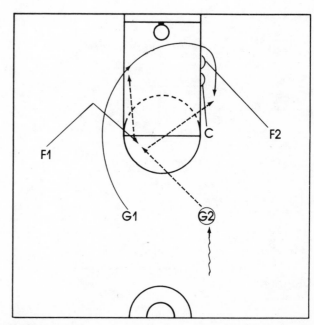

Diagram 2.

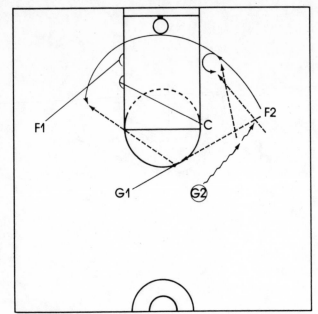

Diagram 3.

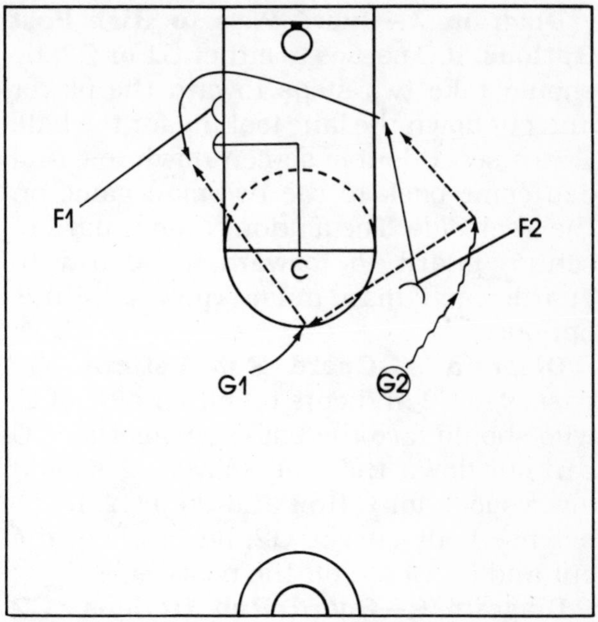

Diagram 4.

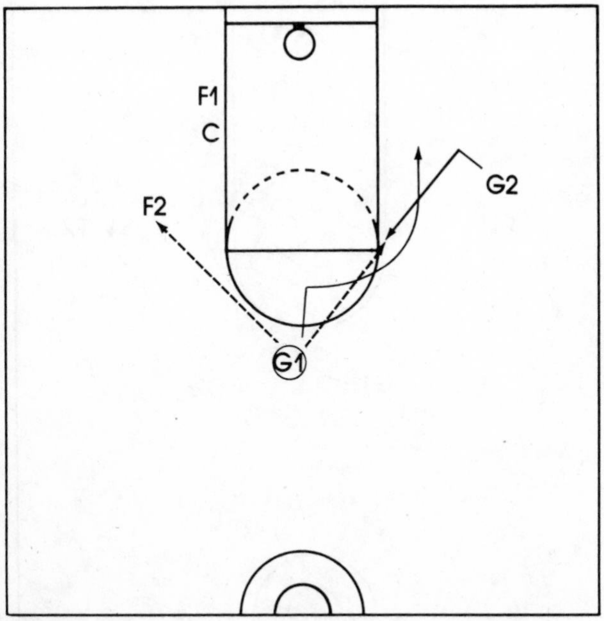

Diagram 5.

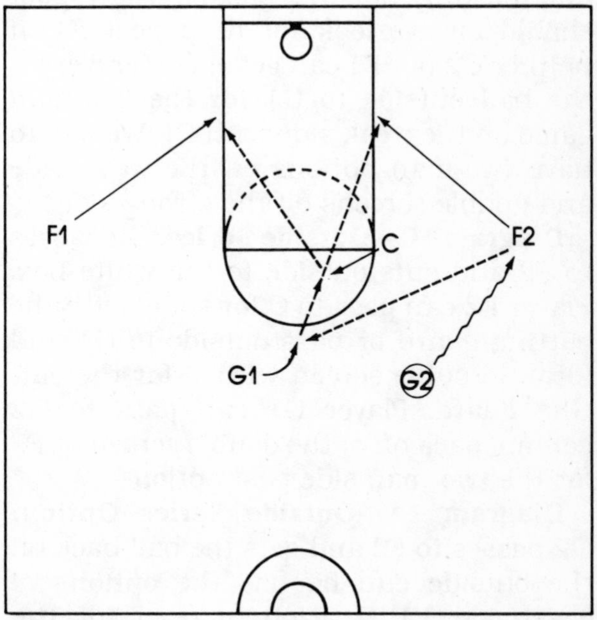

Diagram 6.

Offensive Basics

113

Diagram 7—Guard Pass to High Post Options. If C passes to either G1 or G2, he should take two steps toward the player and cut down the lane looking for the ball. C can set a double screen down low and can come back to the two-man game on the weak side. The motion can be guard to center, guard to forward, or guard to guard; each man must know all three options.

Diagram 8—Guard Rub Pattern. G2 passes to F2 and cuts off either side of C, who should face the basket. Sometimes C can cut down the lane. Player F2 should always look for C first and then G2. If the defense body-checks G2, he can fake the cut and let Gl cut off the post.

Diagram 9—Guard Rub Options. G2 passes to F2 and cuts off C. F2 passes to C, takes two steps toward the ball, and cuts to the basket. If F2 is not open, C should look for G2 coming around the F2 screen and cutting for the basket. High post should always look for deep post F1; if neither G2 nor F1 can get open, C reverses the ball outside to G1 for the two-man game on the weak side with F1. We like to have two-man options on the weak side and double screens on the strong side.

Diagram 10—Outside Series. G2 passes to F2 and cuts outside to the white box. Player F2 can pass to C for splits with the cutting guard or pass outside to G1 and form a double screen with C for the cutting guard. Player G1 can pass to G2 coming back off of the double screen or F2 for the two-man side post option.

Diagram 11—Outside Series Option. G2 passes to F2 and gets the ball back on the outside cut; he has the options of passing to F1, C, a lob, or reversing the ball back out to G1 for the two-man and double-screen options.

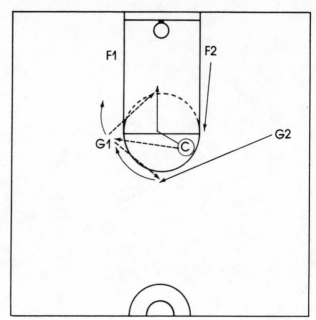

Diagram 7.

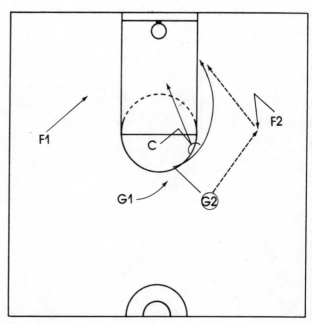

Diagram 8.

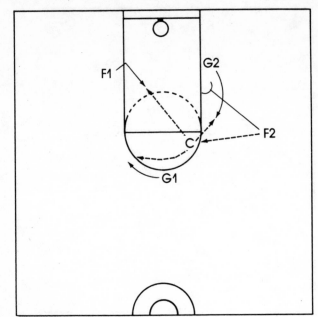

Diagram 9.

Diagram 10.

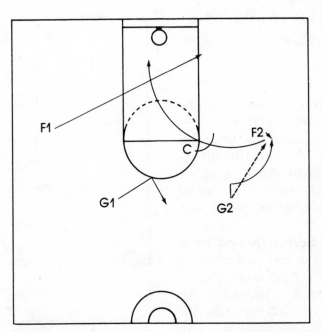

Diagram 11.

Offensive Basics

OFFENSIVE SERIES

C. M. Newton
Vanderbilt University

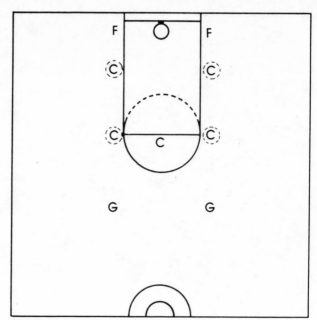

Diagram 1.

We operate out of three offensive alignments: the two alignment *(Diagram 1—single postman can line up anywhere)*; the A alignment *(Diagram 2)*; and the three-game alignment *(Diagram 3)*. We run all our offensive series from these alignments and teach our offensive series out of the two alignment.

Diagram 4—Inside Series (keyed by a direct pass). Player 1 passes to 3 coming to the wing and cuts to the basket. Player 5 moves to the mid-post and looks for the pass from 3. If 5 is not open, 3 reverses the ball out to 2, who has just made a V-cut *(Diagram 5)*. Player 2 looks for 4 and then 5 cutting into the lane. Player 2 can pass to 1, who has the same options *(Diagram 6)*. Player 4 must seal or front-cut his man.

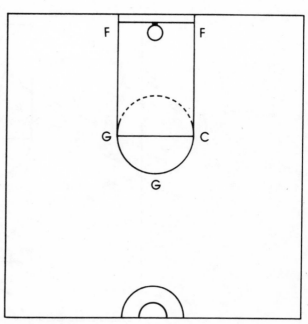

Diagram 2.

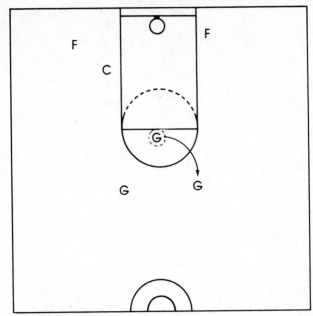

Diagram 3.

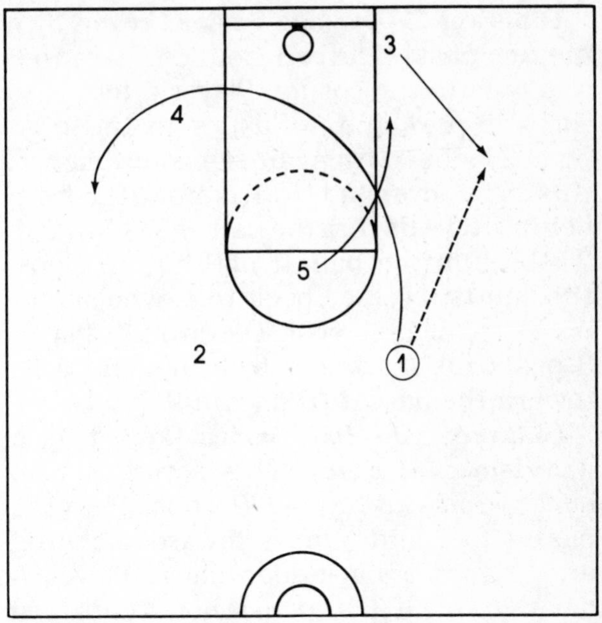

Diagram 4.

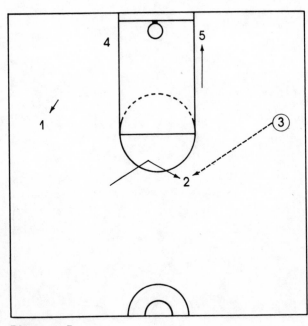

Diagram 5.

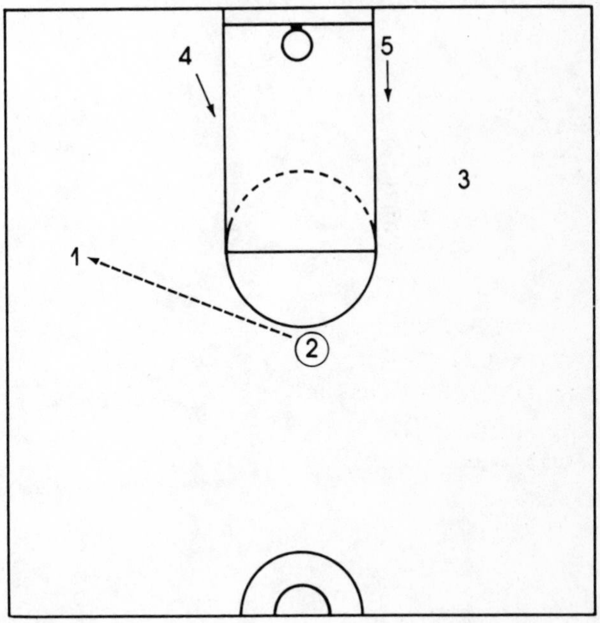

Diagram 6.

Offensive Basics

Diagram 7—Outside Series (keyed by a bounce pass). Player 1 bounces pass to 3 and cuts to the corner. Player 5 moves to the mid-post and 4 flashes to the high post; 2 loops away. Against a zone defense, this is an overload. If 5 is guarded from behind, 3 feeds him the ball; if 5 is fronted, 2 lobs him the ball. If nothing develops, the ball is reversed back to 4, who comes out from the high post *(Diagram 8)*. Player 3 posts his man, and 5 delays and rolls toward the basket *(Diagram 9)*.

Diagram 10—Post Series (keyed by a guard-to-post pass). This series is also effective against a 1–2–2 zone. Player 1 passes to 5 and 3 fakes toward the wing and makes a back-door move. Player 4 delays to see if 3 is open; if not, 4 cuts into the lane. Player 1 can also set a pick for 3 coming to the wing, who then cuts to the basket *(Diagram 11)*.

The A-alignment offensive series is shown in Diagrams 12, 13, and 14.

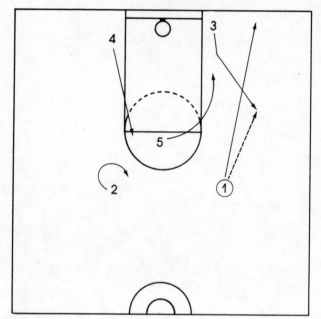

Diagram 7.

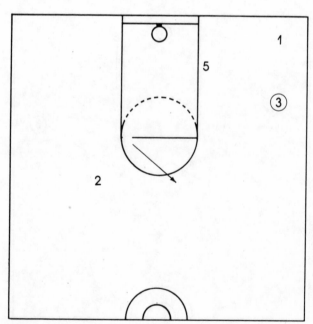

Diagram 8.

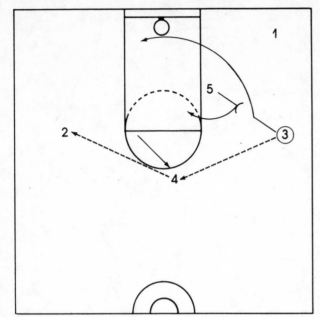

Diagram 9.

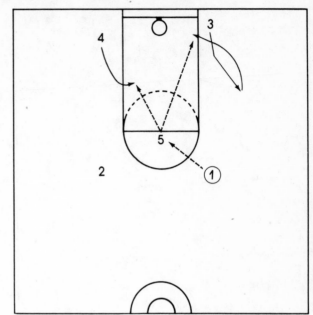

Diagram 10.

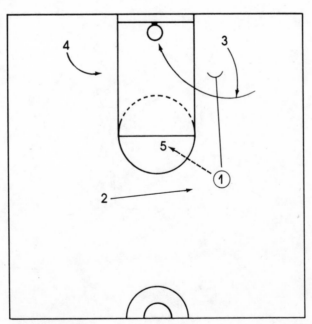

Diagram 11.

Offensive Basics

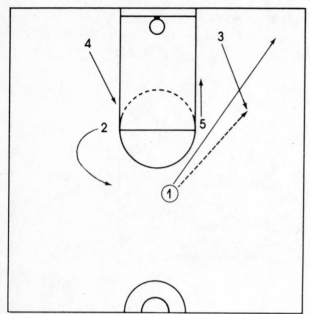

Diagram 12.

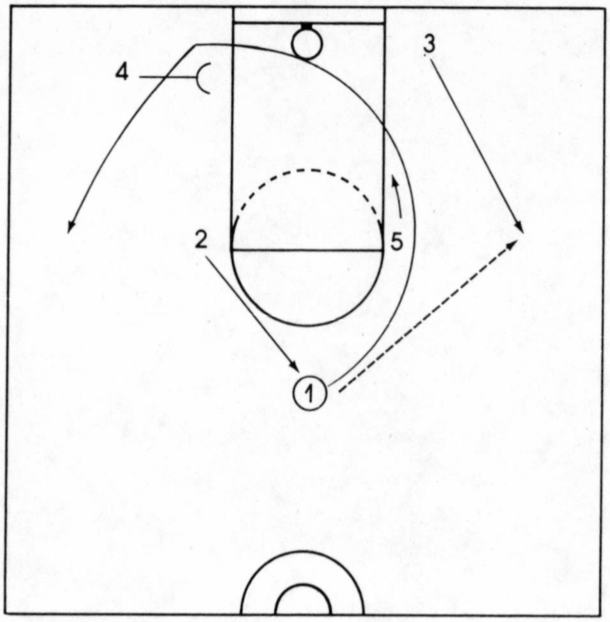

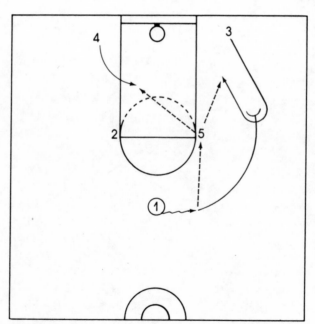

Diagram 13.

Diagram 14.

FAST-BREAK BASKETBALL

Clarence Gaines
Winston-Salem State University

The primary starting point of a fast break is the defensive rebound. From this point, regardless of any other opportunities, the fast break may be employed. The secondary starting point of a fast break is after a completed free throw or field goal.

The outlet pass after a rebound is the most crucial pass of the system. The best passers from the rebound position can pass out right- or left-handed after quickly determining the position of the outlet receiver. The two forwards and the center are the players who must be skilled in this technique. The outlet pass goes to a specified area where a receiver is waiting. Rebounds in the center and the right side of the rebound area are passed to the right (the passer's right when he faces down court); rebounds on the left go to the guard stationed on the left sideline.

The outlet receivers are the guards. Their position varies from the corner baseline area to a position midway between the top of the key and the center line (along the sideline), depending on the power, skill, and rebounding ability of the outlet passers as well as the strength of the offensive rebounders. The more powerful the offensive rebounders, the closer to the baseline the outlet receiver positions himself. The optimum position to prevent guard interference is at a point opposite the free throw line.

The outlet receiver moves to his position very quickly after he briefly blocks out his opponent. His back is to the sideline so he can see the placement of the defense, and he is stationary to present a good target. He must move immediately down court without charging an opposing guard who might be coming in for an interception or delaying action. The best guards for the fast break are good dribblers, especially against a single defender. The guard who can dribble by one defender and thereby cause a two-on-one or three-on-one situation is an invaluable asset.

The guard opposite the outlet-receiving guard breaks immediately down court. He follows his lane to a position near the basket and holds there. His primary function is to make the defense drop back and thereby leave the center open or defended by only one man. Getting the quick pass for a drive-in shot is of secondary importance.

The third man in the fast break is an extremely important part of the system. He is one of the rebounders, usually the one not engaged in the outlet pass phase. As the rebound is secured and before, or quickly after, the outlet pass, he sprints for the third or outside lane on the side of the outlet-pass receiver. He may cross in front of or behind the ball handler as he dribbles to the middle and down court. Very often the outlet passer himself is in a position to follow his pass and becomes the first man in the third lane.

The two remaining rebounders (trailers) may carry out any one of the following assignments: trail the break slowly, protecting the back court; trail the break quickly to an intermediate shooting area for a field goal attempt; drive into the scoring area for a pass from a four-on-three situation (the fourth lane is between the center lane and either outside lane); rush the offensive board after a field goal attempt; move quickly to the regular set offensive position once the fast break has been stopped.

Guards do most of the ball handling. The third man and the center-lane guard do most of the scoring. The center-lane guard is usually the leader in assists. The

Offensive Basics

big men, the rebounders, do not handle the ball in the offense except for quick return passes, a drive-in shot, or an assist. The driving layup is the key shot in the fast break. The driver must score or be fouled in the attempt. The second most important is the shot from the foul circle by the center-lane guard.

The period directly after the fast break is stopped is an interim during which the defense may be quite disorganized and opportunities for scoring are many. Good ball control during this period is essential.

The mechanics of the fast-break offense are as simple as any other offense; however, drills must be devised for each phase. The individual's ability to handle the ball under high-speed conditions requires thorough grounding in fundamental footwork and passing (especially avoiding traveling violations).

Diagram 1—Little Man-Big Man Drill. A single line is formed out of bounds along the sideline at the corner of the court.

Each guard (little man) with a ball has a forward or center (big man) behind him. The guard dribbles the length of the court, shooting a right-handed layup or close-in shot. The forward who trails immediately behind him rebounds (if the shot is missed) and passes out to the guard racing down the right sideline. If the shot is made, the guard will wait along the sideline not farther than the mid-court line for the forward or center to take the ball out of bounds and baseball-pass the ball to him. The guard then dribbles to the free throw circle and passes off to the forward or center, who drives in from the outside lane for a layup shot.

Diagram 2—Little Man-Big Man Plus One. A third player, usually a forward, trails the two as they drive to the goal. He attempts to offensively rebound the ball if the field goal attempt is missed, stop the outlet or in-bounds pass; and plays defense on a two-on-one fast break back to the starting end of the court.

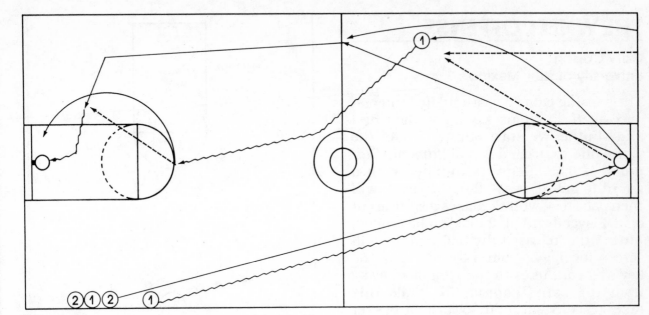

Diagram 1.

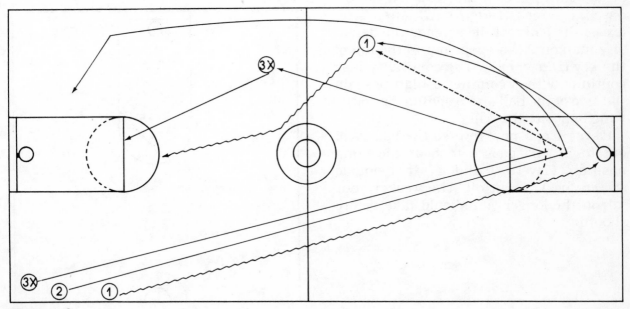

Diagram 2.

Offensive Basics

THE WHEEL OFFENSE

Gary Colson
University of New Mexico

The passing game has stimulated interest once again in offenses such as the wheel and shuffle. We start our version of the wheel offense from a 2–3 alignment *(Diagram 1)*. The offense is initiated with a guard-to-guard pass—2–1. Player 1 will then pass to 4, while 2 makes a shuffle cut off 5. Player 4 will hit 2 inside if he is open. After 1 has released the ball to 4, he will screen for 5, who comes to the top of the key and continues to the wing spot away from the ball *(Diagram 2)*. While this takes place, 3 will cut in toward the basket and come across to the high-post position.

Should 4 be unable to pass inside, he will pass to 5 at the top of the key, who will reverse the ball to 1 at the opposite wing. In the meantime, 2 and 3 set a double baseline screen *(Diagram 3)*. After 5 releases the ball to 1, he screens the defensive man on 2, who pops out to the top of the key *(Diagram 4)*. The continuity may continue with 3 coming to high post on the side of the ball and 5 sliding out to the wing opposite the ball.

Player 1 can now reverse the ball back out to 2, who passes to 5 at the wing position. Players 3 and 4 set a double screen for 1 to cut off. The weaker your talent, the longer you should take before shooting.

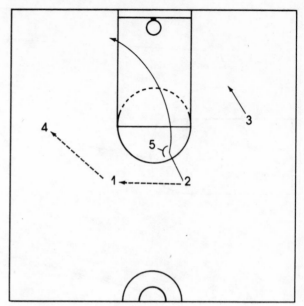

Diagram 1.

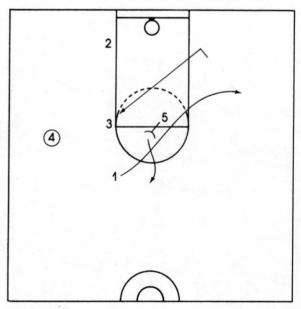

Diagram 2.

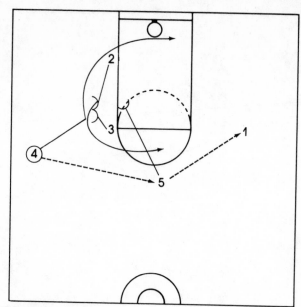

Diagram 3.

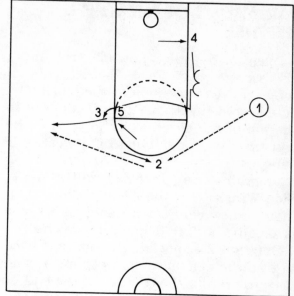

Diagram 4.

Offensive Basics

VARIATIONS OF THE WHEEL OFFENSE

Diagram 5—Stack Set. Player 1 hits 2 and screens away for 4. Player 3 cuts off screen by 4 to the side of the ball to set double screen with 5. Player 5 pops out to the top of the circle ready to reverse the ball to 1 who pops out to the weak-side wing.

Diagram 6—Against Sag on the Weak-Side Wing. From the basic alignment, 1, instead of screening for 5, screens X3, who is sagging off 3 to help out on defense.

Diagram 7—Special. This move is used to trap the defensive man playing 1, who tries to prevent the reversal of the ball by sliding up the middle to the top of key.

Diagrams 8A and 8B—Delay Pattern. From the basic alignment the wing man merely dribbles the ball back out to the guard slot and resets.

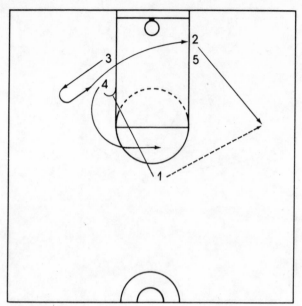

Diagram 5.

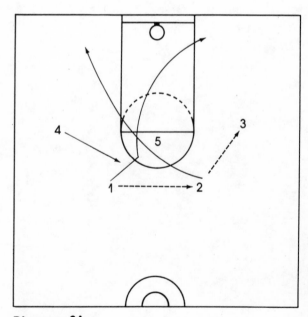

Diagram 8A.

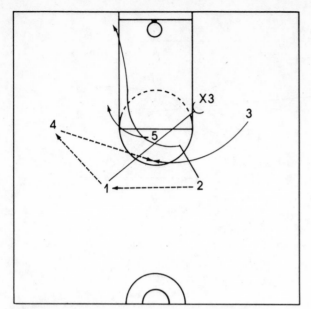

Diagram 6.

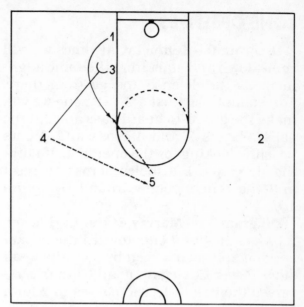

Diagram 7.

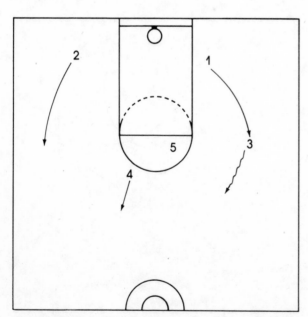

Diagram 8B.

Offensive Basics

ZONE OFFENSES

Diagram 9—Kentucky. At times we will come down and start from the same alignment as the defense and go from there. For example, against a 2–1–2 zone we will make the guard-to-guard pass and cut the gaps. Players 2 and 4 cross and 3 cuts baseline looking for the openings. If nothing develops, 1 dribbles across to reset and the others rotate around *(Diagram 10)*.

Diagram 11—Murray State. In this set, 2 passes to 4 and cuts toward the basket coming around a screen by 3 on the weak side. Player 5 steps out and quickly reverses the ball to 1, who passes to 2 for a baseline shot.

Diagrams 12-14—Palm Springs. Offense is initiated from a 1–3–1 set with 1 passing to 3 at the wing. Players 5 and 4 rotate high-low inside with the ball at the wing position. Player 3 takes a few dribbles toward the corner. If 4 has come across and gone low and is not open, he steps out to receive the pass on the baseline from 3, 3 screens for 5, who steps out. After the screen, 3 continues to the top of the key, while 1 vacates the point and moves to the wing position *(Diagram 13)*. If nothing develops, 4 passes to 1, who passes to 3 at the point *(Diagram 14)*. Then 4 cuts to the middle off a screen by 5. Player 3 can hit 4 directly or pass to 2 who can pass to 4 low or 5 coming high after the cut. Once again, 4 and 5 work the inside rotation with the same options on the other side of the court.

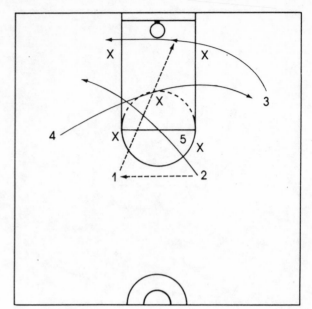

Diagram 9.

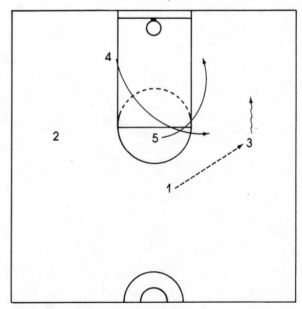

Diagram 12.

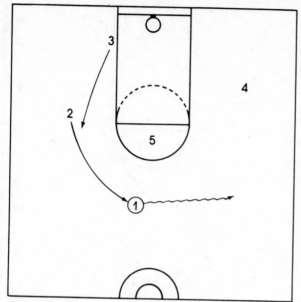

Diagram 10.

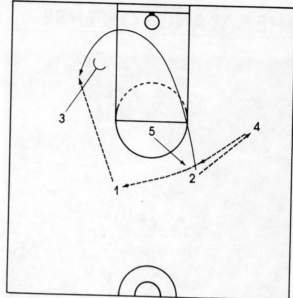

Diagram 11.

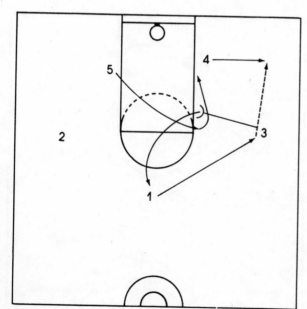

Diagram 13.

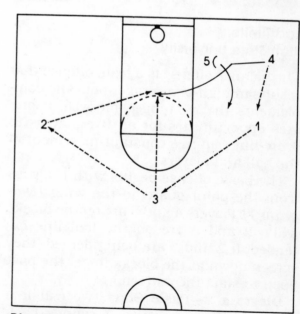

Diagram 14.

Offensive Basics

THE BALANCE OFFENSE

Diagram 1.

Rod Tueller
Utah State University

The balance offense is a team offense that results in high-percentage shots and complements the running game well. It creates opportunities for all five players to score but requires constant movement of the ball and players.

The basic offense begins with the pass from the point guard to the wing *(Diagram 1)*. Players 4 and 5 are on the blocks while 2 and 3 are on the foul line extended. If 2 and 3 are being denied, they screen down at the blocks to get the post open to start the pattern.

Diagram 2—Basic Start. We call it a banana offense because it swings back and forth in the shape of a banana. We start 15 to 18 feet apart with low-post players screening away and flashing back to the ball. Point guard 1 can pass to the wing and screen away.

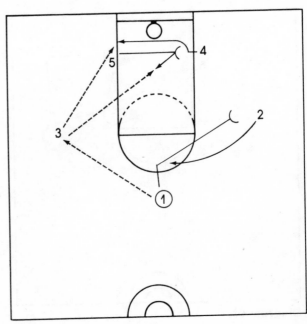

Diagram 2.

Diagram 3—Flash and Flare. Player 5 flashes to the ball strongly, while 4 either flares or stays, looking for the hi-low pass.

Diagram 4—"X" the Post. When the ball is reversed after the post can't get the ball, 3 passes and screens for 2, and 1 looks for either 4 or 5 crossing to the post area.

Diagram 5—High-Post Options. The post area should be passed to at least every fourth pass. Our wing players can float to the open area instead of the interchange on reversal options.

Diagram 6—Point Penetration. On point penetration into the lane, 1 looks

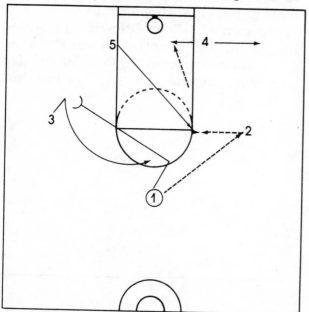

Diagram 3.

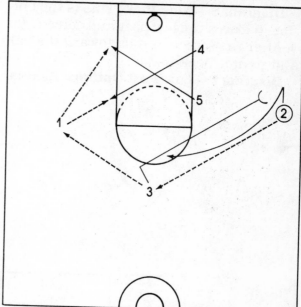

Diagram 4.

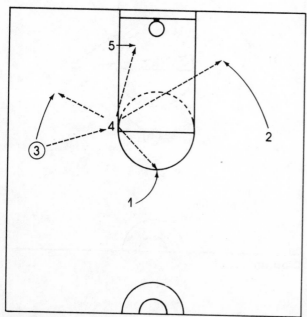

Diagram 5.

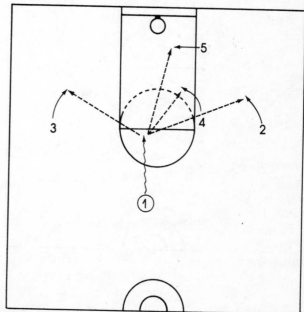

Diagram 6.

Offensive Basics

for the high post sliding down and dumps it off or takes the shot. This works best on ball reversal.

Diagram 7—Screening. Take two to three steps and V-cut back off the screen. You must set your opponent up—this is the most important part of screening.

Diagram 8—Back Pick. This is the only time 5 leaves the low post and screens for 3. After the screen, 5 rolls toward the ball and rotates back inside.

Diagram 9—Low-Post Options. Against a match-up zone, we play a man-to-man offense with the following things in mind: more flashes, quick reverses, fewer screens, more penetration, and more high-post moves.

Diagram 10—Penetration. We dribble to penetrate and fill the gap against both man-to-man and zone defenses.

Diagram 11—Zone Offense. Quick ball movement and penetration are the keys. Draw two defenders and look for the gap and seams for the pass inside or the shot.

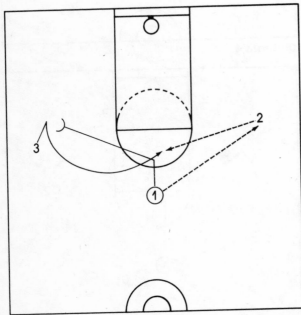

Diagram 7.

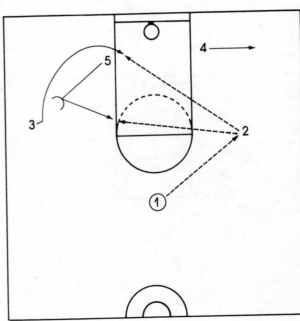

Diagram 8.

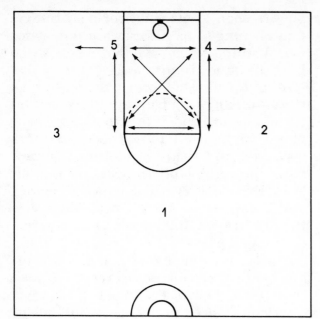

Diagram 9.

Diagram 10.

Diagram 11.

Offensive Basics

QUICK-PASS MOTION OFFENSE

Norm Sloan
University of Florida

Our quick-pass motion offense came about as a result of a shell drill we used in practice. We play four-on-four with no dribbling and the offense was able to score and maintain possession, so I felt this was a good philosophy for our offense.

From the first day of practice we condition our players to pass the ball to the first open man. I used to say five passes or more, but it took the fun out of the game. So now we look for the layup at the first opportunity. In the first 15 to 20 seconds after we bring the ball down the floor, we put the ball overhead and look at the basket.

In a freelance offense like this, it is mandatory that you keep a shot chart because you must prove to the players where the best percentage shot is. I use a shot chart at every practice and game. My players soon know what their shot selection is going to be if they want to play for me. Winning team and shot selection go hand in hand *(Diagram 1)*.

After a made shot we use the fast break *(Diagram 2)*: Player 5 always takes the ball out of bounds and enters to Player 1, our main handler. If 1 is not open, the pass goes to 4 and then to 1. Player 2 always runs the right lane and 3 runs the left lane. Even if they must cross, Players 2 and 3 always run their lanes. Player 4 is the first trailer, and 5 runs to the low box on the ball side.

Against full-court zone defense, we run the break the same way except we may change the end of the break. I believe a good running team that gets the ball in quickly is difficult to press. So we may try this at the end of the break *(Diagram 3)*: Player 4 comes down the floor and goes to the low post on the ball side. Player 5 goes to high post on the same side. If 2 is overplayed, 2 and 3 will cross; 3 could go high or low. We could also run a high-post exchange.

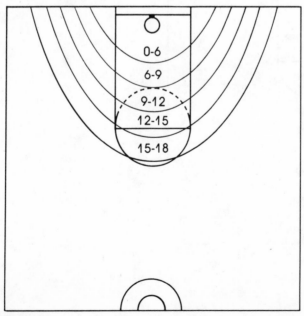

Diagram 1.

We also run our quick-pass motion offense after set plays. I believe you need set plays, particularly at the end of a game. You can play this offense with weak players. In fact, the weaker the players, the greater the need for this offense.

The basic rules are pass and move. Don't stand and watch—make a cut to the basket. You'll find that you need well-conditioned and gutty athletes to run this offense. My players exchange positions and use touch passing to stimulate movement.

My point guard stays off the point and plays to one side. He is not a designated defensive safety valve—everyone knows to get back on defense.

I do not have breakdown drills for two and three players. I believe in total team organization.

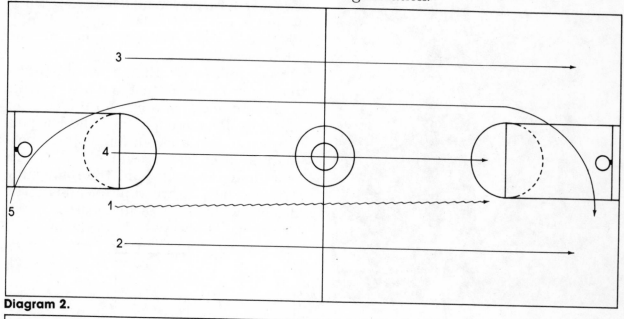

Diagram 2.

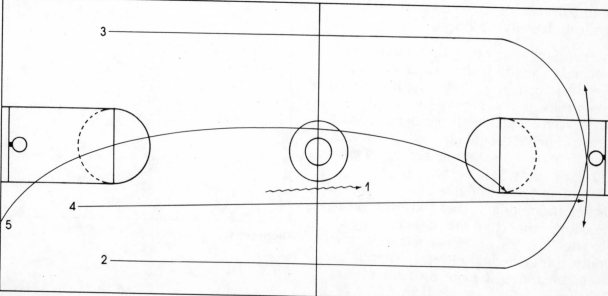

Diagram 3.

Offensive Basics

DOUBLE-STACK OFFENSE

Gene Sullivan
Loyola University-Chicago

The primary weapon of the double-stack offense is the jump shot, the most explosive weapon in the game. The jump shot forces the defense to play tighter; a tight man-to-man defense is vulnerable to a fake and drive. A defender will frequently need help on a one-on-one against a good ball handler and shooter.

Movement in the double-stack offense is toward the middle rather than the flank, the wing rather than the corner *(Diagram 1)*. This creates a wide perimeter with plenty of room to maneuver. It spreads the defense, making it more difficult to double-team.

DOUBLE-STACK MANEUVERS

Diagram 2—Roll. Low man initiates the offense: 2 and 3 jab-step inside and roll around 4 and 5.

Diagram 3—Pull. Low man initiates the offense: 2 and 3 jab-step inside and start to roll but pull to the wing.

Diagram 4—In. High post initiates after slap from low post: 4 and 5 go between the two defensive players. If defense switches, 4 and 5 roll up the lane for the ball. If defense stays, they roll around underneath.

Diagram 5—Out. High post initiates after slap from low post: 4 and 5 step to the wing and low post steps up the lane for the ball. Roll and pull for the low-post players and in and out for the high-post players. The defense will decide for us what maneuvers we run. The tighter the defense, the more we want roll and in. The defense will need to switch more to cover. Players must always look for the ball.

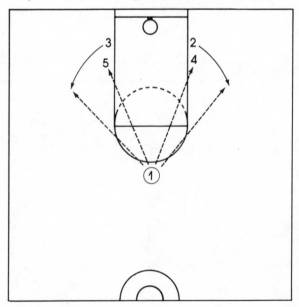

Diagram 1.

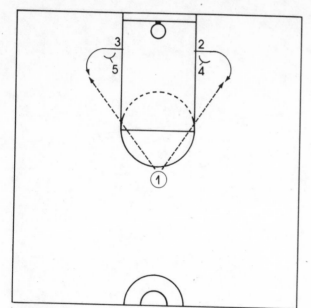

Diagram 2.

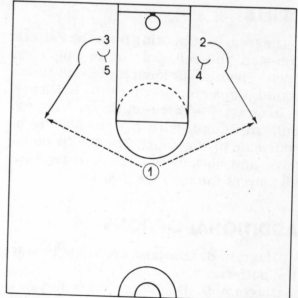

Diagram 3.

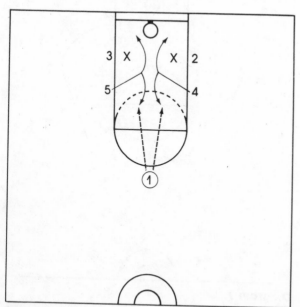

Diagram 4.

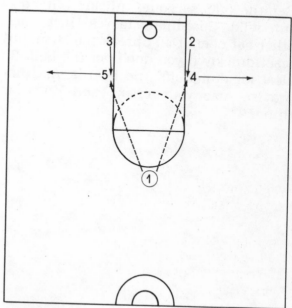

Diagram 5.

Offensive Basics

DRILLS

Diagram 6—Shooting from the Pattern. Jab-step and roll, pull, in, or out to get open. Shoot a stationary, pull-up, turnaround jumper, or take it to the basket.

Diagram 7—Three-on-three. Run roll, pull, in or out, with players staying on your side of the court. Start with no defense and work up to three-on-three. Have all players interchange positions.

ADDITIONAL OPTIONS

Diagram 8. Low-post exchange to start the pattern.

Diagram 9. Double or clear for good shooters.

Diagram 10. Deep set for point guard one-on-one penetration.

ISOLATION OFFENSE TIPS

Get the offense going quickly but don't run wild. Coordinate moves—help each other get open. Don't break too soon, but reset quickly if you don't get the ball. Be alert for dump-offs and boards. And improvise—use your talent and do your thing.

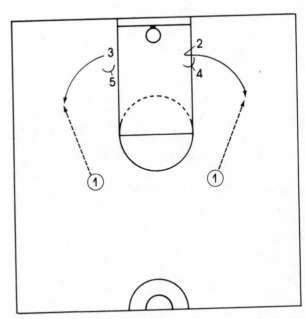

Diagram 6.

Diagram 7.

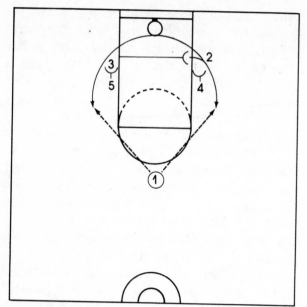

Diagram 8.

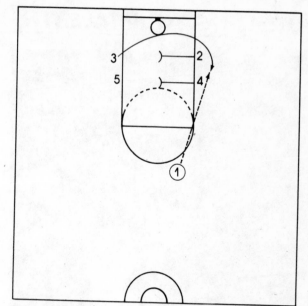

Diagram 9.

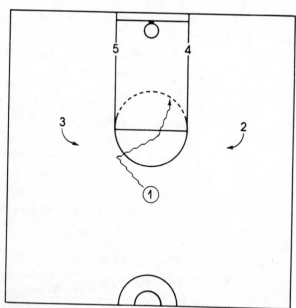

Diagram 10.

Offensive Basics

UTILIZING YOUR TALENT

Denny Crum
University of Louisville

In our high-post offense, we play the center high because we do not want the low-post area congested *(Diagram 1)*. Also, my centers are not big so I want to take advantage of putting my forwards and guards in this area as much or more than my center. Our whole offense is designed to run people into this area and post them up in one-on-one situations. We try to get our shots from the six areas that are shown in Diagram 2. The dotted triangle on each side of the court we call our triangle of success. We work hard to get the ball into these areas.

There are many ways to take advantage of the talents of certain individuals on our team. We have had many players—Darrell Griffith, Jerry Eaves, Rick Wilson, and Junior Bridgeman—who played guard for us but were forwards in high school and played down low with their backs to the basket. So we decided to take advantage of this and get them the ball in the low-post area.

Here are some ways we get the ball to our big guards from our high-post offense. In our back-door series *(Diagram 3)* we look for the lob pass first; if it is not there, we pass to our weak-side forward who then looks for our guard posted up on the block. Another option is to pass the ball to the strong-side forward and cut both guards to the block area on both sides of the lane *(Diagram 4)*. The strong forward then passes the ball to the high post and screens down for the on-side guard, who comes off his screen looking for a jump shot. The high-post center looks first for the off-guard who posts up, then for the guard cutting off the forward screen.

This has been a very good series for us in recent years. The key to success is to have the weak-side help positioned to allow the guard to be one-on-one in the low-post area. If the guard who goes back-door is full fronted, we lob over. If he is side fronted, we get the ball at what we call the weak-side low position. Because most defenders are taught to play man and the ball on a low-post player, we have our guard move under the basket to attract the defender and then step in front and pin the man behind him. This has been very successful for us in getting the ball to the low post.

You must have offensive options that will be determined by what the defense does. If the defense does not allow you to do certain things, you must adjust. The easiest teams to beat are the ones that cannot make adjustments. We use a switching, man-to-man defense because we feel it can take away our opponent's first couple of offensive options. If they

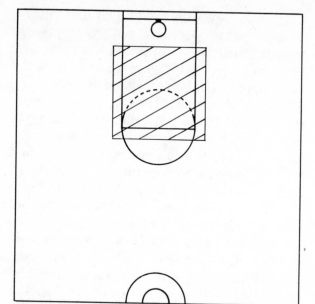

Diagram 1.

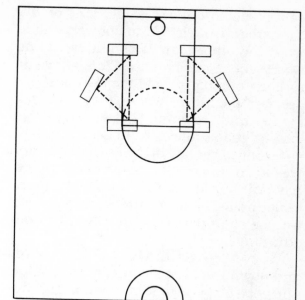

Diagram 2.

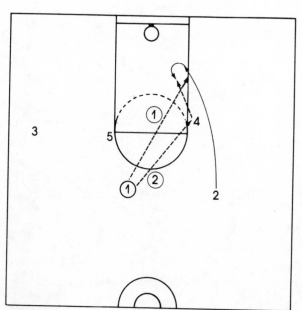

Diagram 3.

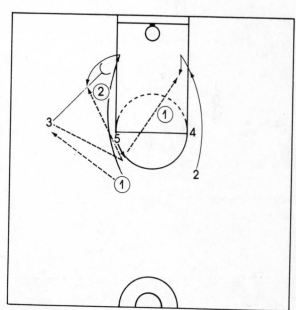

Diagram 4.

Offensive Basics

cannot go to options three, four or five, they are in trouble. We do not worry about what the other team does and we do not worry about mismatches. This allows us to keep our big people in positions they are familiar with, where they can help better and rebound better than our guards. It also allows us to get our guards out front to get our break started quicker. We like to run and it is to our advantage to have our guards in a position to get to the outlet areas. This is another way we feel we use the talents of our players to our advantage.

We want to get the ball off the boards and down the floor as quickly as possible and get a 50 percent shot. You don't always have to run a pattern to get a 50 percent shot; you can get it off your transition game if you practice it. Teams who run

and shoot are often called undisciplined, and we have been called that by some people. But if you practice running and shooting every day, your game play is not undisciplined. You must play like you practice; if you do that you are a well-disciplined team, regardless of your style. The key to the transition game is for each player to know his good shots. You don't want players who can only score from 10 feet shooting 20-footers. Only one team in my first eleven years at Louisville has shot under 50 percent for the season.

Diagram 5 shows our position at the end of the transition break. Player 1, our best ball-handling guard, dribbles the ball down the sideline and tries to get it to 4 in the corner. He is our best-shooting guard and should be able to get there first. If he is open, he shoots; if not, he looks for 5,

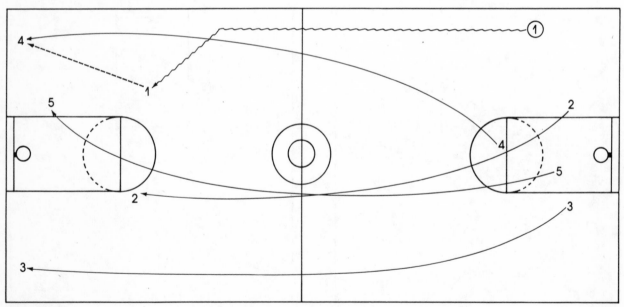

Diagram 5.

our center. Our centers are fast and can beat the other team's center down the floor. Obviously, the center should also be a good scorer in the low post. Also, the defense usually has its guards back and this can cause a mismatch to our favor. Player 2 is our forward on the side the ball is rebounded and 3 is the off forward. On the break, both of these players must get to areas where they can score.

We try to get the ball to 5 whenever possible. If we cannot, we reverse the ball and still try to get it to 5, who tries to pin his defensive man. If the defensive men covering 2 and 3 sag, we pass to them for jump shots. As the ball is reversed (*Diagram 6*), 5 sets screen for 4, who comes off the pick to low post. This type of transition offense gives a chance to take full advantage of our players' talents. We run this off both missed shots and made baskets.

The transition game is best suited to teams that switch on defense, which keeps their players in the areas where they can get the ball and go with it. Against teams that have a very good transition game and don't switch, we cut both of our guards to the low post to take away this part of their offense. Switching allows us to keep our guards out and ready for the fast break. This is probably the main reason we use a switching defense.

Let me add that our switching defense does not get much credit, but if you check the stats you will find that only two or three teams on our schedule shoot above their season's average against our defense. We have led our conference in defensive scoring average the last three years.

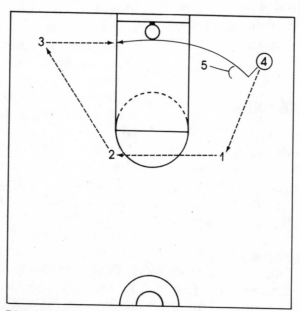

Diagram 6.

Offensive Basics

VIRGINIA TECH'S FAST-BREAK ATTACK

Charlie Moir
Virginia Tech

The keys to successful fast-break basketball are speed and control. Speed becomes a liability rather than an asset unless it is controlled. An excellent way to teach and to improve on controlled speed is through fast-break drills. The success of the fast break depends on the ability of the offense to take advantage of the defense before it can get organized. This latter, or secondary, phase of the fast break, is one of the finest offensive attacks in basketball.

In order for a team to be effective with the fast break the players must be drilled to recognize the opportunities offered by this style of play. If the opportunities do not develop, the fast break should not be forced. Your players must want a *great* shot, not just a good shot. If the great shot is not available, then go into the set pattern.

ADVANTAGES OF THE BREAK

1. Leads to uncontested layups.
2. Results in excellent 15-foot shots while the defense is in transition.
3. Produces offensive rebounding opportunities.
4. Is an exciting, enjoyable brand of basketball.
5. Is a game breaker—most games are won with a two-minute blitz of four or five buckets. The chances of a fast-break team doing this are much greater than those of a control team.
6. Requires that a team be aggressive and well conditioned.

DISADVANTAGES OF THE BREAK

1. Causes more turnovers, as it is obviously more difficult to control the ball going at top speed.
2. Consumes a great deal of practice time.
3. Can lead to more low-percentage shots, especially from selfish players.
4. Has a tempo that is more difficult to control.

SITUATIONS LEADING TO FAST-BREAK OPPORTUNITIES

Interceptions. The fast break starts while a team is playing defense; consequently, a good fast break team must tie the defense in with the fast-break offense. The interception is the best opportunity for the fast break because it immediately puts the man who intercepted the pass ahead of his man. After a steal, a quick solo or two-on-one usually develops.

Diagram 1—One-on-One Drill. Player 1 attempts to score on X1. Both offense and defense are stressed. Player 1 should make his move fast. X1 tries to force 1 into a bad shot or to delay him until help arrives. After a score or missed shot, 1 becomes defensive man and X1 goes to the end of the offensive line.

Diagram 2—One-on-One with Trailer. Same as Diagram 1 except 2 waits until 1 gets to top of circle area and then trails the play. Player 1 either shoots or passes off to 2 if X1 commits on him.

Diagram 3—Two-on-One Drill. Offensive men 1 and 2 attempt to storm the one defensive man X1. Players 1 and 2 run approximately 15 feet apart. The first one who has the opportunity to drive to the basket does so.

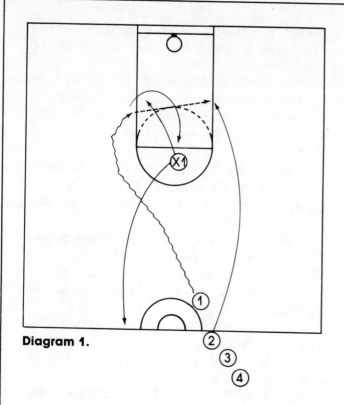

Diagram 1.

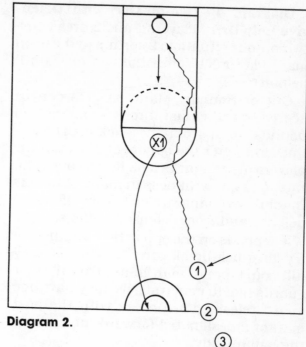

Diagram 2.

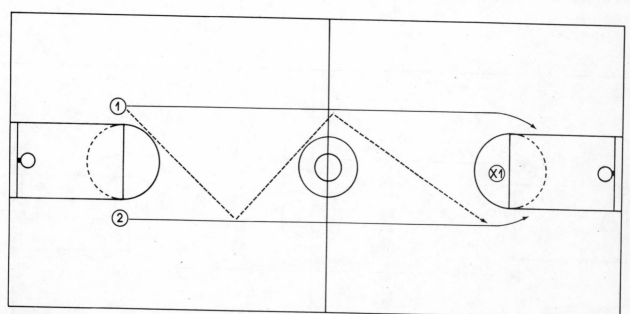

Diagram 3.

Offensive Basics

Diagram 4—Two-on-One with Defensive Help Drill. Players 1 and 2 break on a two-on-one situation; 2 sprints to the open man. Player X1 zones the two men until help arrives.

Out of Bounds. Many baskets can be scored on the fast break from out of bounds, both from the back-court side-lines and after the opponent scores, if the players are taught to look for the opportunity. A major weakness in many players is inability to change quickly from offense to defense and from defense to offense.

It depends on the opposition whether we try to quick-break after a score. If they full-court press man-to-man or if their guards like to penetrate, we may have one guard release down court with the post man or a designated forward inbounding the ball quickly.

At all times we encourage our guards to push the ball up the floor quickly with the forwards and center sprinting to their respective positions; the guards should not have to hold the ball and wait for them.

Free Throws. A scored free throw sets up the same situation as a scored basket. However, we do sometimes run a special quick break following a successful free throw.

Diagram 5—Quick Break Right or Left.

Jump-Ball Situations. If there is any doubt about who will get the tip, play for possession only.

Defensive Backboard Recoveries. These offer more fast-break opportunities than any other situation; therefore, many of our drills are geared to defensive backboard recoveries.

The fast break is built through drills. These are also conditioning drills; a good fast break team has to tie conditioning in with strategy.

Diagram 6—Three-Lane Break (no defense).

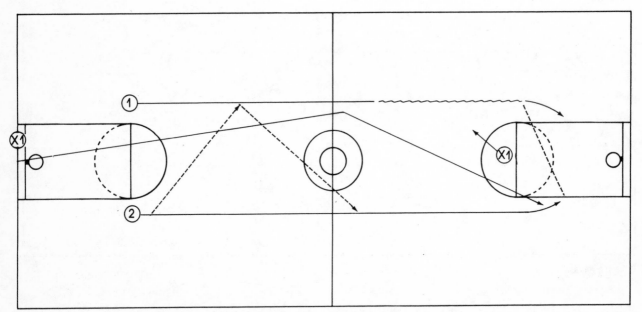

Diagram 4.

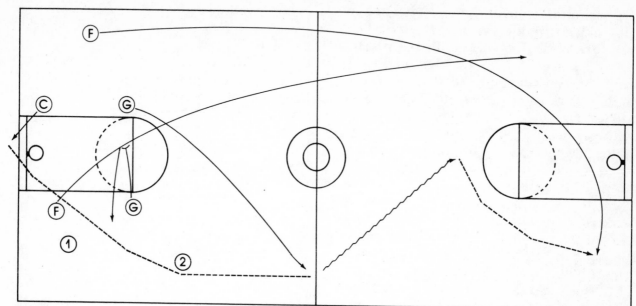

Diagram 5.

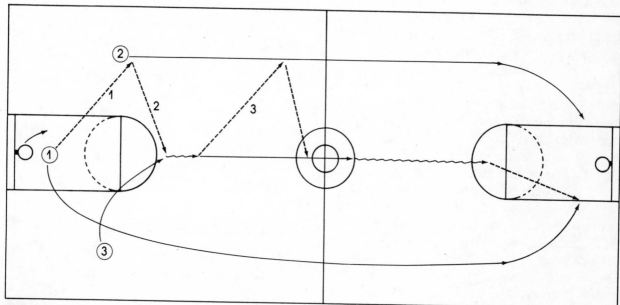

Diagram 6.

Diagram 7—Tail End of Fast Break. As the wing men 1 and 2 enter the vicinity opposite the free throw line extended, they converge to the basket area but never penetrate farther than the inside rebound positions on the free throw lane. The middle man does his passing early, his driving or shooting late. He penetrates to the free throw area—no deeper—forming a 15-foot triangle. They hold this position until the middle man decides whether to get the ball to a wing man on the break of

Offensive Basics

the basket or, if he can get the defense to split, drive through the middle himself.

Diagram 8—Five-Lane Break Drill. Player 1 tosses the ball up high on board. Once he has touched the ball, 4 and 2 double-team him and try to prevent the outlet pass. Once he is able to get the pass by these men they become offensive team-mates. Players 3 and 5 fill the outlet zones for the pass from 1 or the rebounder. Player 5 should get to the top of the circle about five strides ahead of 1, who always comes out the middle. Player 3 passes to 5 as soon as possible and continues down the floor in his lane. If he beats 2 to this lane, 2 holds up and becomes a trailer; if 2 wins the race, then 3 becomes a trailer. Player 4 should fill his lane before 1 can cut over into it; if, however, 1 can fill the lane first, he does so. Forwards can gener-ally beat the center to the wing lanes, so the center trails the middle lane by 15 feet.

So 5 has the middle, 3 the left wing, and 4 the right wing, the first wave of the break. Player 1 trails the middle lane; 2 trails the left wing and moves over to trail 1 by a similar distance. Player 2 has defen-sive balance responsibilities and should not let any opponent get behind him. Player 1 always goes to the offensive basket. If the first wave men hold up at the designated areas 15 feet apart, the sec-ondary phase of the fast break develops.

Diagram 9—Secondary Phase of Fast Break. This is not a drill but an illustra-tion of the secondary wave of our fast-break pattern. Player 4 has the ball (it could be 5 or 3) but doesn't have a good shot, so he looks for 1 trailing the play and cutting into the open area under the basket. This is one of the finest options off the fast break: 4 may get a short jump shot if the defense doesn't declare on him; if he does, 1 is under the basket for a tip or a rebound.

If 4 does not shoot or pass to 1, he will

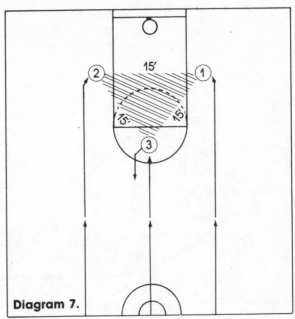

Diagram 7.

look immediately for 2, who has trailed the break. Player 4 pivots and passes to 2, who can shoot or pass to 1 on the post or 5, who moves to the top of the circle as 1 cuts to the basket. Player 3 moves out from the basket about 15 feet; if 5 gets the pass from 2, he may pass to 3.

Thus the ball has gone quickly around the horn and the team is in the set pat-tern game. The fast break blends into the set pattern so that it is very difficult to tell where one ends and the other begins.

FAST-BREAK POINTERS

1. Don't run away from the ball unless the defense attempts to pinch off passes.
2. Screen off the boards and form re-bound position. Every player has de-fensive responsibilities until he or a teammate has possession of the ball.
3. First pass out is the key pass to initi-ating the break—two-handed over-head pass is best to clear the ball out.
4. Guards should screen off the boards, rebound long, and fill the outlet

zones. They should get themselves in the open for the first pass out.

5. The ball should be advanced to the middle as fast as possible.

6. Pass to the man ahead of the ball as soon as passing lane is open—don't wait to make the pass.

7. Players should hold up in 15-foot tri- angle position unless there is an opening to go all the way to the basket.

8. Player with the ball should make the defense pick him up.

9. Use deception in ball handling and playmaking. Be clever but not careless.

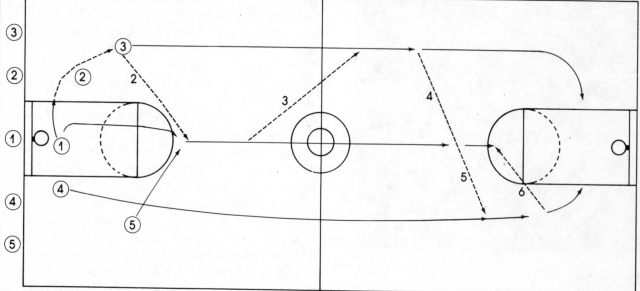

Diagram 8.

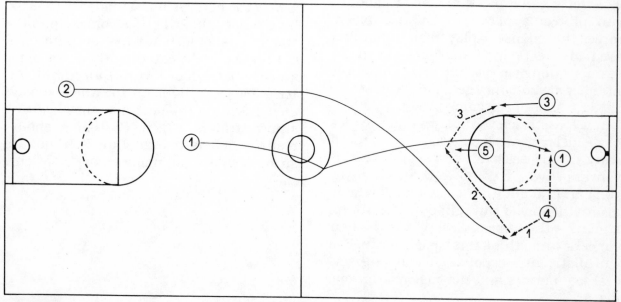

Diagram 9.

Offensive Basics

THE DELAY GAME

Bill Foster
University of Miami

The delay game has many advantages. It can protect a player in foul trouble. It forces the defense to play in an unfamiliar area of the floor. It disrupts the other team's offensive rhythm and limits the number of shots they get. And it can set up the last shot of the game.

You have to sell your players on the idea of the delay game. It's a good idea to use it early in the season, even against teams you know you're going to beat. This way you can find out what some teams will do against it so you can refine it. The Miami stall uses the same philosophy as the four corners, and I think it is easier to run. You can distribute responsibility among several key players and not just rely on one player.

The post players should line up at an angle so the wing players lining up behind them can see the court better and have a better angle to the bucket. Keeping the stack wide leaves the middle of the court open for the one-on-one. Most of the time we will use our normal lineup but sometimes we'll insert a third guard. Late in the game we try to get our best free throw shooters on the floor. The perimeter people are the most active, and the post men do not get involved that much, but they must be alert for opportunities to back cut to the basket.

As 1 comes down the floor, the stack should stay tight. After he makes his move to one side of the floor, passes should be no longer than 8 to 10 feet *(Diagram 1)*. Stolen passes in this area often result in uncontested layups. Every time the ball handler passes to a perimeter man he makes a banana cut to the bucket; the wing player with the ball must give him two or three seconds to get open near the basket *(Diagram 2)*. The banana cut makes it difficult for the defender to double up on the ball. When 1 finishes his cut, he replaces wing player 2 in the stack.

Now the defense has a tendency to relax. If he senses this when he comes up to the stack, he should plant his foot and back cut immediately, catching the defense for an easy back-door layup *(Diagram 3)*. After a few repetitions of this, the defensive men guarding the post men may begin to stand straight-legged. Post men should read the defensive man's knees; if they are straight he should make a back-door cut.

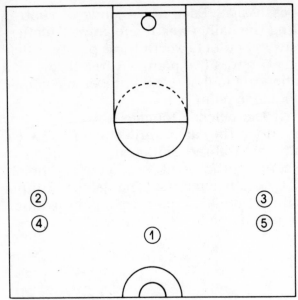

Diagram 1.

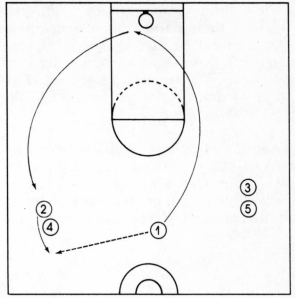

Diagram 2.

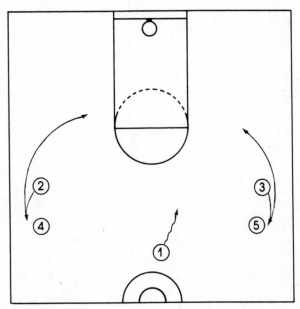

Diagram 3.

Offensive Basics

This delay game is most effective against a tight man-to-man defense; however, it cannot be used against a trapping defense. Whenever we encounter traps in this delay, we simply "square it" *(Diagrams 4 and 5)* and get the ball to the middle of the floor.

Ahead-and-Behind Drill. Two teams alternate playing offense and defense for two minutes at a time (the game clock makes this drill more realistic) using an additional point system based on time of possession. Each 15 seconds of controlling the ball is worth one point. An offensive rebound is worth three points. A field goal counts five points. A free throw on a shooting foul is five points; on a common foul, one point.

If the defense touches the ball in any manner, they are awarded a point. A steal is worth three points, and if they can score on the break or secondary break, they get five points. (The defense cannot run set offensive patterns.) Taking an offense charge is worth three points.

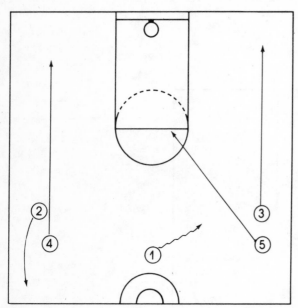

Diagram 4.

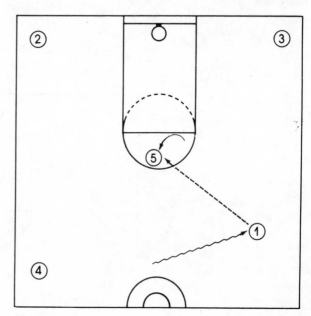

Diagram 5.

ZONE OFFENSE

**Murray Arnold
Western Kentucky University**

Our zone attack is designed to create maximum, efficient movement against various zones, match-ups, and combination defenses. Such movement includes cutters, dribble penetrations, post-ups, and slides into open areas. After installing our basic attack, we found that certain simple modifications made it more effective against specific defenses. After presenting our basic attack, we will show these easily incorporated modifications.

In order to assure an easy entry that will guarantee early ball and personnel movement, we start from a 2–2–1 spread-out alignment.

Diagram 1. Guards are at a 12-foot spacing to assure easy passes between them if needed. Forwards are at the foul line extended to make easy initial guard-forward entry passes a reality. Center is preferably on the block opposite the ball as the guards initiate attack.

Diagram 2. On the guard-to-forward pass the off-guard cuts to the ball side short corner and the center posts up on line between the ball and the basket. This creates a basic 1–3–1 alignment.

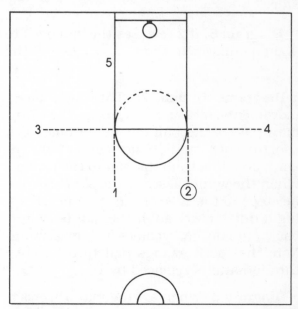

Diagram 1.

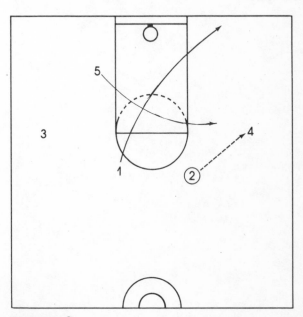

Diagram 2.

Offensive Basics

Diagram 3. On any pass from the wing back to the point, the passer cuts through to the basket and the short-corner man replaces him at the wing.

Diagram 4. If 2 swings the ball to 3, then 4 moves to the short corner on ball side.

Diagram 5. If 2 reverses the ball back to 1 then 4 moves to the short corner on the ball side.

Diagrams 6 and 7. Therefore, basic movement rules are: Any time the wing man passes the ball out he becomes the short-corner man. The center always stays on a line from the ball to the basket. When the wing passes to the short corner he steps to the edge of the foul line, creating a quick overload. If the ball is swung back outside he becomes the new wing. Note that as 2 swings ball to 3 he cuts through and is replaced by 1.

Diagram 8. When a wing man throws a skip pass he cuts through to the short corner.

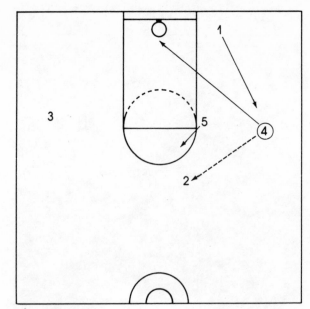

Diagram 3.

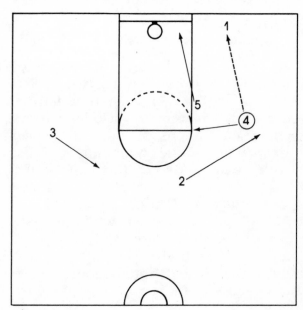

Diagram 6.

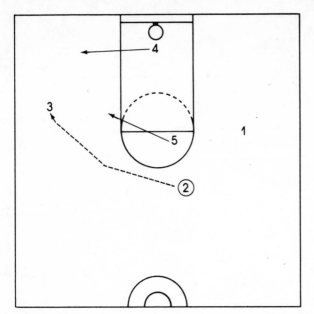

Diagram 4.

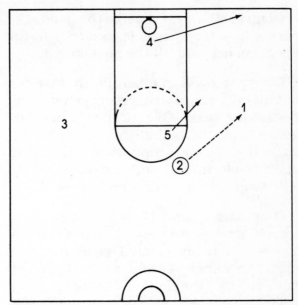

Diagram 5.

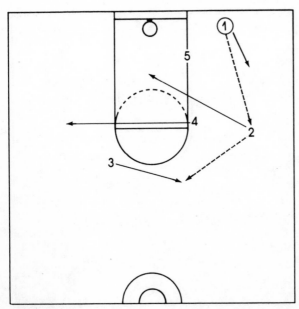

Diagram 7.

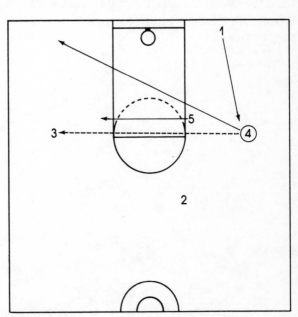

Diagram 8.

Offensive Basics

Diagram 9. But if you like the inside "X" action it is very possible to dive 5 to the short corner and fill the post with 1.

Diagram 10. It is essential that we not fall into the trap of neglecting penetration toward the basket. We encourage our players to drive the ball at the zone, particularly the second time they handle it. Against odd-front zones we have found the following dribble action very effective.

Diagrams 11 and 12. If this is done the second time a wing man handles the ball we have already created good ball and player movement. Obviously this opens up both sides of the floor. If 4 skips to 3 and cuts, 3 can look inside or continue action by driving the ball into the other side of the zone.

Diagrams 13 and 14. Encourage drivers to look back to open people, particularly when driving the ball toward the middle of the floor.

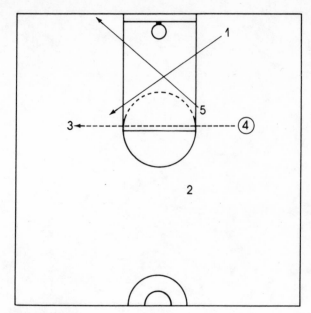

Diagram 9.

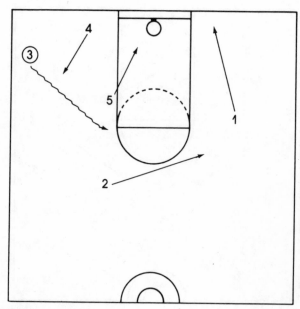

Diagram 12.

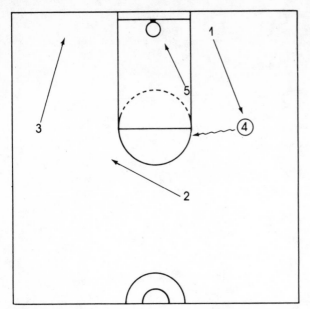

Diagram 10.

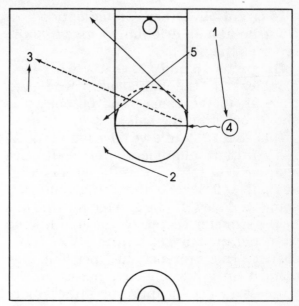

Diagram 11.

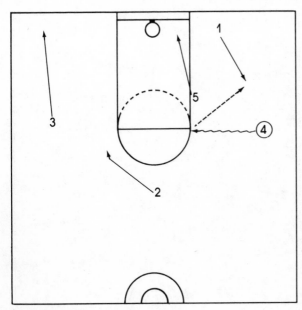

Diagram 13.

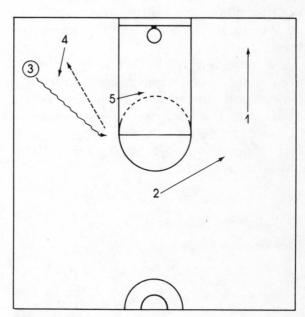

Diagram 14.

Offensive Basics

Diagram 15. Other dribble options include point man dribbling out a wing who replaces the point.

Diagrams 16 and 17. Or the wing man dribbles out the point man, who goes through to the basket and becomes the short corner on the ball side.

Diagram 18. While we have found the 2–2–1 initial alignment very effective against odd-front zones, it seems that against a 2-3 zone the initial cuts are somewhat slow. So we started putting our best perimeter scorer on the foul line so we could quickly get him to either short corner. His presence at the foul line opened up initial effective passes to the wings and got us into our attack more quickly.

Offensive rebounding is quite effective as cutters are in an excellent position to get to the glass. Also, short-corner men have good angles for sneaking to the boards. Whoever is filling the point area checks back defensively to prevent the break.

We have found that shot selection is greatly enhanced when players wait until the second time they handle the ball to penetrate the defense. Such restraint guarantees good ball and player movement and encourages aggressive individual attacks on the zone.

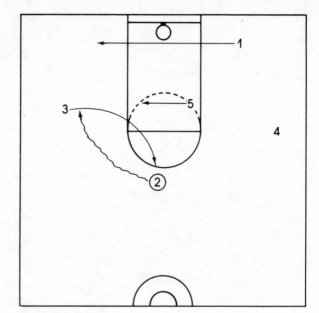

Diagram 15.

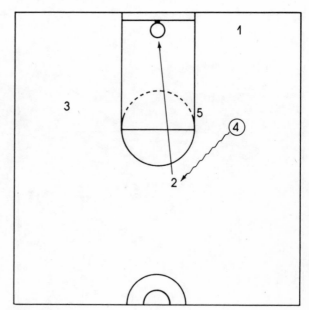

Diagram 16.

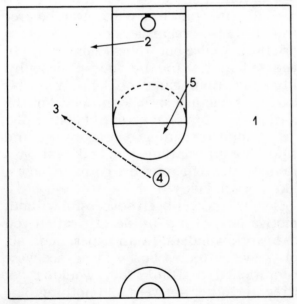

Diagram 17.

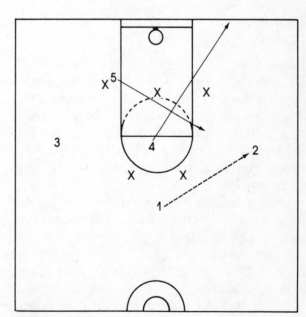

Diagram 18.

Offensive Basics

THE COMPLETE COACH

Dale Brown
Louisiana State University

What does it take to become successful? Be yourself. Two of the most successful college basketball coaches in history—John Wooden and Adolph Rupp—have completely opposite personalities. You must have a flexible personality, but you must coach with your personality, not someone else's.

Have confidence in your own technical ability and experiment. Just because you're not at some high-powered college doesn't mean you can't coach. Let your own abilities come out through your team.

Keep it simple with constant repetition. The first and last law of learning is repetition; 85 percent of what you learn today will be forgotten within 48 hours. You will retain almost 70 percent of what you listen to if you hear it at least six times. Don't overcoach or make it complicated—there are no secrets.

Teach discipline. You've got to have several forms of discipline. One form is teamwork. It's not just enough to talk about it; you've got to implement it on the floor, put the team above yourself. Whenever I see something in a newspaper or magazine about teamwork, I post it in our locker room. I bring in outstanding athletes during the season to talk about teamwork. Another form of discipline is good shot selection. C. M. Newton puts different-colored dotted lines on the floor for guards and forwards to remind them where their shooting ranges are. Another form of discipline is team defense. Another is superb physical conditioning.

Be firm and consistent but coach with a positive attitude. Don't have two sets of rules; otherwise, respect will begin to disappear. Firmness also involves a little bit of love. I don't want to dehumanize my players.

Everyone has to expect and learn to accept criticism. You will never be free from criticism, regardless of your success or effort. You've got to have confidence in yourself and stand by your philosophy. After the final game of John Wooden's career, a victory over Kentucky for the national championship, one of John's biggest supporters hugged him in glee and said, "Congratulations; you had us all worried. We thought you were going to blow it like you did last year."

No one has ever been successful without motivation. With genuine motivation you can work wonders. In an experiment, six of twelve runners chosen for a race were conditioned to think they wouldn't get tired; the other six were told nothing. The experimental group placed first through sixth in the race.

Don't be afraid to fail. Albert Einstein and Leonardo da Vinci both said that 90 percent of their experiments ended in failure. But they persisted.

Know yourself. Who am I? Where am I going? What do I want? Buddha said that before man can ever find happiness, he must know himself. You can fake it, but deep down inside you've got to really know who you are or you'll fall along the way.

What makes Johnny run? What motivates us? What motivates John Wooden, Lawrence Welk, the president of General Motors? All these men who have been highly successful have said that what has driven them to the top was a feeling inside of wanting to do something besides being great, of knowing themselves and wanting to make the world a better place to live in.

I'm convinced that you can motivate your athletes. You have to be reasonable but they can do more than they know, and all of us can go to the top.

APPENDIX: BASKETBALL CAMPS

A good way to hone your basketball skills is to attend one of the many college and university basketball camps run throughout the country each summer. You will learn basic techniques from top-notch college players and coaches and compete with other aspiring basketball stars. If you attend camp, be ready to work hard because it's serious fun.

BASKETBALL CAMPS

All-American Basketball Camp
Utah State University
Logan, Utah 84322

Murray Arnold's Basketball Camp
Western Kentucky University
Bowling Green, Kentucky 42101

Dale Brown's Basketball Camp
Department of Athletics
Louisiana State University
Baton Rouge, Louisiana 70894

Gary Colson's Basketball Camp
University of New Mexico
Albuquerque, New Mexico 87131

Denny Crum's Basketball Camp
University of Louisville
Louisville, Kentucky 40292

Bill Foster's Basketball Camp
University of Miami
Coral Gables, Florida 33124

Bill Frieder's Basketball Camp
University of Michigan
1000 South State Street
Ann Arbor, Michigan 48109

C. E. Gaines's Basketball Camp
Winston-Salem State University
Winston-Salem, North Carolina 27110

Howard Garfinckel's Five-Star
    Basketball Camp
58 Seminary Avenue
Yonkers, New York 10704

The Georgia Tech/Bobby Cremins
    Basketball School
Georgia Tech Athletic Association
150 Third Street
Atlanta, Georgia 30332

Walt Hazzard's Basketball Camp
UCLA
405 Hilgard Avenue
Los Angeles, California 90024

Terry Holland's Basketball Camp
University of Virginia
Charlottesville, Virginia 22903

Bobby Knight's Basketball Camp
Indiana University
Assembly Hall
Bloomington, Indiana 47405

Bill Leatherman's Basketball Camp
Bridgewater College
Bridgewater, Virginia 22812

Charlie Moir's Basketball Camp
Virginia Polytechnic Institute
    and State University
Cassell Coliseum
Blacksburg, Virginia 24061

C. M. Newton's Basketball School
Vanderbilt University
Department of Athletics
2601 Jess Neely Drive
Nashville, Tennessee 37212

Johnny Orr's Basketball Camp
Iowa State University
Hilton Coliseum
Ames, Iowa 50011

Roanoke Basketball Camp
Director-Ed Green
Roanoke College
100 College Avenue
Salem, Virginia 24153

Norm Sloan's Basketball Camp
University of Florida
Gainesville, Florida 32604

Sonny Smith's Basketball Camp
Auburn University
Auburn, Alabama 36831

Norm Stewart's Basketball Camp
University of Missouri
P.O. Box 677
Columbia, Missouri 65205

Gene Sullivan's Basketball Camp
Loyola University of Chicago
Chicago, Illinois 60626

Paul Webb's Basketball School
Old Dominion University
Norfolk, Virginia 23508

PHOTO CREDITS

All instructional photography by Tim Trevilian, Roanoke, Virginia. Other photos courtesy of Duke University Sports Information; University of Louisville Sports Information; UCLA Sports Information; University of Alabama–Birmingham Sports Information; Auburn University Sports Information; Louisiana State University Sports Information; Midland Junior College; Virginia Tech Sports Information; University of Miami Sports Information; Vanderbilt University Sports Information; Indiana University Sports Information; University of Michigan Sports Information; Winston-Salem State University Sports Information; Georgia Tech Sports Information; University of California–Santa Barbara; Loyola–Chicago Sports Information.